To Faith,

Thank yc

Thank for all you do and your
strength to share your
own story!

ESCAPING MY
PREDATOR

A TRUE STORY

BY MARY J SCHALLA

Mary J Schalla.

◆ FriesenPress

Suite 300 - 990 Fort St
Victoria, BC, V8V 3K2
Canada

www.friesenpress.com

ISBN
978-1-5255-9818-0 (Hardcover)
978-1-5255-9817-3 (Paperback)
978-1-5255-9819-7 (eBook)

1. BIOGRAPHY & AUTOBIOGRAPHY, PERSONAL MEMOIRS

Distributed to the trade by The Ingram Book Company

Table of Contents

Chapter One

MEETING MY PREDATOR

I DIDN'T KNOW it at the time, but in July of 2014, my life changed.

On July 6, 2013, I posted a picture of myself on my private Facebook profile page; I was wearing a little black dress and sitting up against a wall in a sexy pose, in a bar with a friend of mine, a night we really needed. After posting this picture, I received a personal Facebook profile message, something many of us do, from someone I did not realize was quietly watching my page, unseen and unheard until he announced himself with one comment, "With a picture like that you'd better be careful."

That's all it took to engage me in a conversation. All it took was someone to give their attention, liked how I looked, and made me feel pretty. This one comment led to hours of conversation and messaging back and forth, starting with a game of truth or dare, and early morning meetings when my shift ended and his begun. Hours and days of him putting me on a pedestal, treating me like a princess, and making me feel sorry for him because he was going through a separation, and I knew what that felt like. One comment that, without me knowing it, led me, a naïve 31-year-old woman, to my predator.

I was nearing the end of a divorce, one that was not messy, but still fresh, and we both still had some hurt feelings. I was just learning to be on my own, a single mother of two. I had a good job with a great schedule, working security. I had been training my body hard to apply for the Edmonton Police Services, something I have always wanted to do. I was running seven kilometers a day, sprinting the last kilometer, doing weights, and swimming daily. I had all my paperwork ready to send off. I was ready to do the physical part of the test after spending countless hours at the gym. I had taken my firearms courses and updated my CPR and first aid. I felt I was ready!

Then my predator came along and I allowed him to redirect my focus. He told me he wanted to spend more time with me. He told me he wanted me to work fewer hours at night. He asked me to find another job. I won't lie. I fell for him. I fell hard. Everything seemed like it was going in the right direction—that we could do anything if we were just together. Not everything was his fault; I should have taken more time to get to know him. I should have taken things a bit slower, but I had worked with him a couple of years before this and thought I knew him pretty well and could trust him. I should have gotten to know his family better, gotten to know his history, but at the time, it didn't seem to matter much, as he seemed pretty open to answering all my questions.

When talking about his family, only one thing seemed odd to me, but not like an out-of-place odd, not something that would catch one off guard. He mentioned that his sister no longer spoke with his family. He never really gave a reason for why they never spoke, but because my dad didn't speak to his brother for years, I didn't really think about or get into why she never spoke to them. What did she do? This was the only question that came to mind. The question of what did *they* do never entered my mind until later. My predator said he did not have the best childhood. His father died when he was young; he had a crappy stepfather who he did not get along with, and he had done drugs of all sorts, and he drank alcohol.

My predator worked his way into my life unexpectedly, and very quickly got me to fall in love with him. It was like we were meant to be, a puzzle that just fit together. Things seemed okay. We were both happy. As with many relationships, we had a great honeymoon period. After a few short weeks, he told me he loved me. He moved in on November 1, 2013 after he told me he needed to move out of the home that he was still sharing with his now ex-wife. He wanted to talk about moving into my place and living together to start our lives. He introduced me to his children when we took them tobogganing. He introduced me to a friend of his who we later found out was a family friend of my father's from a long time ago. She and I clicked, too. She even asked me to come over and have a movie night. I thought it was great making a new friend. I couldn't help but think, *yes, a girls' night would be awesome.* I had not had many of those girls' nights after starting to date my predator. We were each others focus.

My new friend and I had our girls' night. I was so excited, and at the time, my predator seemed happy that we were hanging out. He told me to have fun. I did. We had a movie night at her house, and chit-chatted about girl stuff, getting to know each other, and finding that we had some things in common. We got along fantastic! What I didn't know was that after my girls' night, I would be faced with my angry boyfriend. During the evening, I was getting text messages asking when I would be home. I replied, "I don't know, when the movie is over, it's

3

a girls' night, could be late." When I got home, he was mad. He didn't ask me if I had fun, he asked me why I was out so late. I looked at him, amazed, thinking, *Seriously... didn't you introduce me to your friend to be friends?*

I thought I could avoid an unnecessary argument; I told myself to go to bed. He followed me upstairs to our bedroom, giving me the silent treatment: He did, however, feel the need to tuck me into bed. Then he left the room and slammed the door behind him. I lay there, not moving, wondering what I did wrong. *Why was he so mad?* I didn't understand. This was just the first of many things I would tuck away in the back of my brain, thinking I had done something wrong. The next morning he apologized for his behaviour; he said he didn't know why he was so mad. This would be the first of many apologies that were to come.

My predator told me about his ex-wife. He told me things that made me want to stay away from her, things that made me scared of her. I never got to know her personally, just through him. He made it sound like she was at fault for their divorce; that she cheated on him, wanted a polyamorous relationship. He told me that she had asked to have coffee with me one on one, and he said that he would not allow this to happen, and told her that he had to be there. I became scared of her, knowing only what my predator told me. I didn't feel like, after the things he told me about her, she and I should ever meet alone. It took almost three years before she and I even said hello to each other. That's all it ever was, a decent hello. My guess is that he was telling her nasty things about me so that she wouldn't want to meet me, either. At some point, we both just gave up the idea of ever getting to know each other.

There are so many forms of addiction. I thought those that physically changed your appearance or changed your personality, like drugs, were the only kinds of addiction, as I have never been subjected to anything, really, other than alcohol or drugs. I lived a pretty sheltered life as a child. My parents protected me as much as possible from the realities of the ugly world. I only became aware of alcohol and drugs because my ex-sister-in-law had a problem with both from a very young age. I didn't know that porn and the need to have sex constantly were also considered to be addictions.

Most relationships have a "honeymoon" period, and ours was no different. Other than being introduced to watching porn more than occasionally, I thought we had a pretty normal sex life. I suppose porn is still kind of taboo, and not many people talk about it openly, but my predator did not have a problem talking about porn or his needs or wants for sex. I have nothing to hide and nothing I am ashamed of. In this new relationship, I just thought porn was something that I was supposed to be interested in as a sexual being. I was also curious, and because he enjoyed it, I thought I should try, too. I had watched it once before but I was not really into it. Like I said, I was naïve. Until the age of 25, I didn't know that masturbating was considered "normal," and that this was something people did.

He slowly introduced the porn he liked to watch. At first, it was not enough to scare me away; only enough to be curious about what I was watching—curious to try something new. The porn started off light and soft, and turned hard and dominant. I didn't realize it was a real problem until I became pregnant in March of 2014. We had planned this baby together because we were in love, because my predator was older than me by eleven years, and if we were going to have a baby, now was the time to do it. While pregnant, I of course became quite tired, and most nights, I just wanted to sleep. Quite often I would be awoken by the TV in our bedroom going quieter. I would lazily open my eyes to my predator lying beside me, masturbating to porn. I made sure not to move because if I did, my predator would quickly make the move on top of me to shove his already hardened penis inside me.

I learned quickly, while I was pregnant, that if I woke, not to move—stay silent and take slow breaths. If I didn't and he caught me, he immediately took that as a cue that I was up because I wanted to have sex. He told me how he loved pregnant women, how sexy pregnant women were, and that he had an odd obsession with pregnant women. Just one more clue I missed. I was just excited that we were having a baby together.

I found it strange that his nine-year-old son also enjoyed watching porn, like it was no big deal. His dad casually checked his son's internet history one day to find his son was watching Mario porn. When his dad confronted him about it he explained to his dad that it helped him masturbate. Because his son and five-year-old daughter still shared a room in our home, he told his son he could not masturbate in a room where his sister was sleeping. That it needed to be in private and with his door closed so no one would walk in. Shortly after that, I decided it was best for him to have his own room in the basement. I couldn't figure out why a nine-year-old would even know what porn was. I asked my predator how old he was when he first started to masturbate. He told me he was around the age of ten. He told me that, at the age of sixteen, he and his guy best friend experimented on each other, sucking each other off to see what it felt like to have someone give head. I didn't understand that. Perhaps it's no different than girls wanting to experiment. I have no clue, as that was not something I was into at the age of 16.

My predator also found the need to send me pictures of himself, often jacking off. Sometimes these pictures would be taken while I was at work, sometimes they would be taken while he was at work and in his office, and sometimes he would send me random pictures of porn, in hopes we could try it some day. In the beginning of our relationship, I didn't mind his pictures. I even sent him pictures of myself, which has become a common thing between couples. What I didn't realize was that my pictures could and would be posted publicly on social media for all to see, after I went to the police for help.

This is a lesson I learned the hard way, but perhaps I can stop it from happening to just one person—one person who has complete faith and trust in the person with whom they share these intimate photos. Realize that when you leave an abusive relationship, or any relationship that sours, the person you once completely trusted can turn around and post your intimate photos online. Should this happen, also realize that this is a criminal offence and the person can be charged.

Not all signs of his addiction were prominent at first—it took time to make their appearance. I couldn't figure out how such a huge personality trait could not be the most dominant part of someone. I stressed over how I could have missed the signs; how I ignored the signs. I am realizing now that, day-to-day, it didn't have to be dominant, but just easily hidden when you're with the right person; someone who brushes it off as weird, but not enough to make them leave. Enough to show there is some kind of personality difference, but not enough to give a clue that it's much worse than what you can see. Perhaps I was just ignorant, and ignored all the signs that were clearly in front of my face. I don't know. I just knew things had changed.

Chapter Two

NO CONTROL

MOST PEOPLE HAVE this idea that relationships need to be equal in order to work. That both need to make around the same amount of money, or if one makes more the other will make up for it in housework or by helping more with the kids. That you take turns sleeping in. That all household chores are equally balanced out between the two people. Sadly, this is not reality. One or the other will start to feel the pressures of the other's lack. They will argue more, they will go silent, they will separate because they have stopped communicating, and then divorce, because they are angry with each other. My predator and I seemed to be able to talk about anything, or so I thought. He told me he would never lie to me. He told me he would never lie to my parents.

I didn't realize that I was slowly starting to lose control of my identity. Who I was becoming was not who I had wanted to be—who I was raised to be. I was losing myself and being moulded into this other person I didn't know. My predator, I believe, enjoyed my suffering—financial, physical, and mental. My predator told me he wanted to take care of me. Many abusive spouses control the financial aspects of the relationship. This was not what I thought was the case with our relationship. I was the person who looked after the family. I paid all the bills. He didn't have a bank account so used mine. Got my predator's vehicle registered and paid his phone bills. I was the one who worked seventeen-hour days for nearly three years. My predator lost his job, for one thing. He stayed home. He told me he was looking online for work, but when I saw him on his phone, he was playing games. He told me he had applied to many places, but that no one had responded. I couldn't help but think, *how can someone put out so many resumes and hear nothing for almost a year?*

My predator also said he wanted to start his own painting company. I was supportive and told him that if that would make him happy, then I was on board. My predator had no motivation for work. He never advertised a business to paint, relying on his friends to get him jobs, because he was too lazy to put a simple ad on Kijiji or Marketplace. Not having a job didn't make him less horny, however. His focus changed to more sex. He was home now all the time, so he felt he could get it any time of day. He groped me in the kitchen, standing behind me while I leaned against the island in the kitchen, and dry humping me from behind, grinding his penis into my ass, sometimes while the kids sat at the table and ate. I would push him off and go do laundry, or clean something. My parents kept asking me if he had heard anything from any of the job applications he was sending out. They also found it hard to believe that no one had responded to him. I felt the need to defend my predator, believing that he was applying, but I just didn't see him doing it for myself. My dad finally talked to a friend's son who was hiring. My dad got him a job. My predator had an hour lunch break with this new job. He never used to come home on his breaks, but when he started working this new job he came home every day. He would rummage through my drawers, and he left my vibrator on after checking to see if I had used it while he was not home.

My bath became a time where he felt the need to invade me, and he pulled the curtain fully open to watch me in the water naked and stare at me. Sometimes, he would pull his penis out and start masturbating while looking at me in the water, inching closer to me hoping I would want to wrap my mouth around him to finish him off. Sometimes that didn't feel like it was an option. I was becoming so uncomfortable around my predator. I felt like my body was no longer my own.

After having my son, I applied and got a new job. My predator started getting angry with me when I got a promotion at work. I was working longer hours because I wanted that next step up the ladder, and it wasn't far if I worked hard. He started asking me why I was working so late, who I was with, who I was messaging, and he became jealous of my life away from home. I got to a point where I would rather be at work. Working at least meant I was not being touched when I wasn't in the mood, being forced to give head, or watch him masturbate. Even though I worked long hours, my predator expected sex. He thought it was okay to be beyond reasonably exhausted and still meet his "needs." I gave no indication of interest in sex when I was so exhausted and unwell, which was a lot of the time. I am sure this would frustrate any person sexually, but if he had loved me, he would have understood that I was working hard for him, for the kids, for us. He would have understood that I was not taking care of myself, and allowing my health to decline, because I knew that if I didn't work so hard, we would have no home and no food for the kids.

I didn't even realize all the things that were changing. I used to go visit my family in Calgary often. I used to go out with my friends or have people over. I was outgoing and friendly. Over time, my visits lessened. My calls to my family and friends slowly dwindled, and when I did call friends or family, I made sure to do it when my predator was not home. If I saw him pull up, I was quick to let the person go by saying, "He's home—I gotta go." All I had was work, my kids, and my predator. Not knowing or realizing what was happening myself, no one else could tell that anything was wrong. Regardless of what was happening at home, when we were around people, I was "happy". I smiled, I chatted, I interacted. The people I talk to now had no idea what was happening behind our closed doors.

Financially, we never had enough left over to do things with the kids. Even working three jobs, I barely made ends meet. I was frustrated. I didn't understand why he wouldn't fight his ex-spouse about his excessive spousal support payments. Why he never fought to have more time with his children. Why his then 13-year-old son, when asked if he wanted to have more time with his dad, told his mother, "No, I don't want to spend any more time with him;" something my predator told me. My parents helped where they could, and I used the money they gave us towards the bills or to buy food. I wonder where my predator thought that money was coming from?

I became physically and mentally exhausted from trying to keep up with all the household bills, his smoking habit, looking after the kids, and keeping up the household chores. I had very little help. Physically, my body started to give out on me. Mentally, I was exhausted, thinking about how else I could earn money to keep us from sinking and becoming homeless with five kids. He didn't seem to care how tired I was. He played off my exhaustion, making me feel bad for him because "he was struggling" financially with the payments he had to make to his ex for spousal and child support payments. I refused to make those payments. He managed to contribute around four hundred dollars a month towards household bills and rent once he finally went back to work.

He was constantly borrowing money from his family but the money would disappear. My predator would accept it and spend it all, never adding it to help pay for bills or for rent or food. He even borrowed money from his ex-wife at times without telling me until he had to pay her back. If there was any money in my bank account, my predator would spend it. I don't know how his family didn't get frustrated with his lack of motivation. I am grateful I never signed any papers with him except a lease which thankfully was able to be broken. If you are fleeing an abusive relationship you can break a lease. I never opened a bank account with him or added him to my account. I owned both vehicles, but he was the main driver on one. It was an easy switch to just give him the vehicle he mostly used as it wasn't worth much. I kept my vehicle.

A friend of mine came out to visit us from New Brunswick in the fall of 2015. She wanted to treat me to a night out. She wanted us, she and I, to go to a casino and rent a hotel room for the night, and have a girls' night. I was stoked! I had been working so much, and I needed this break. Low and behold, my predator lost his mind. "Why do you need to stay in a hotel when you live in the city?" "Why can't you just come home?" "Why do you need to be away from home?" "What are you going to be doing there anyways?" I didn't understand why he was so angry about me staying in a hotel for the night. I asked him if it would be different if I left the city for the night and stayed in a hotel. He said, "Well no, not really." I didn't get it. I stood my ground and told him I was going.

This manipulative behaviour went on for a week. The entire week my friend was there. I asked him if I ever gave him a reason for not trusting me. He said no, and apologized for his behaviour, telling me that he had his own insecurities, and it was his problem to deal with. This was not the first time I heard these words. He never really spoke to my friend the entire week she was there. I am sure this made her super uncomfortable. He texted me constantly throughout the day to see what my friend and I were doing. He wanted to know every detail. My friend didn't like him. She didn't tell me this until much later. Our whole night at the casino, I was forced to answer my phone when my predator messaged or called. It was often and it was annoying. My best friend was concerned for me.

Chapter Three

THE LOSS

IN MARCH OF 2014, I was overjoyed to learn that I was expecting. I could not have been happier that I was about to expand my family and blend it together. Although I had had rough pregnancies before, including one miscarriage, leading to a dilation and curettage the next was a healthy pregnancy, but my oldest son came early, and he ended up in NICU for a week because of his fussy breathing, and then one more pregnancy during which I was on bed rest at five months, and vertigo that lasted right till my delivery day, I was still excited to do it one more time.

Little did I know that my little man would make things more difficult for me. Before twelve weeks, I found out there was bleeding around the placenta. They put me on bed rest and said I could miscarry him. At thirteen weeks I was told to continue my bed rest as he was still threatening to miscarry, and my hips had separated early to the point that I was not able to walk. Throughout my pregnancy I was bound to either a couch, a bed, or a wheelchair, not knowing if my baby would make it to full term. At 38 weeks my water finally broke. With all the stress of not knowing if my little man would make it till to 38 weeks, I felt overwhelming joy when he arrived safely, and was put into my arms. The doctors told me that I should not have any more children. They told me that if I became pregnant again they would take it. It was too much of a risk to carry another baby, both for me and for the baby.

For myself, I never thought abortion was an option. On Dec 29th, 2015, I took a pregnancy test, which I was certain would turn out to be negative. The shock when those two pink lines showed up right away was beyond words. In fact, I was at a total loss for words as the shock ran through me. I was finishing the end of my night shift at work when I bought the test. I thought I should just do it before going home so I wouldn't have to worry my predator. I was in awe when the test came back a complete positive; I went to my friends before going home to my predator. I guess it shouldn't really have been a surprise. My predator didn't care if he came inside me, even knowing the risks. My predator even told my doctors after having our son that I was not having any procedures done to prevent ending up pregnant again. Maybe I should have gone home to my predator first, but I didn't know what to say. I thought talking to my friend would help clear my head of the things I didn't want to think about; the only option my doctors had given me at the end of my last pregnancy. I didn't want to have this talk with my predator. We knew what the doctors had told me during my last pregnancy. I did not want to deal with what would have to occur over the next few months. So I went to my friend. She was shocked, too, and of course, she asked me what I was going to do. At first, I told her I was going to keep it. Then, I said I did not know. I knew what the doctors would say, but I really didn't want to hear it. I wanted this baby, and I didn't care that my life could be at risk.

When I did eventually go home, I somehow could not spit the words out to my predator. Instead, I went straight to bed. I slept very little, and thought a whole lot. I pondered every single thing. I already had three children who needed me, but this little being growing inside me also needed me. I was not only a mother to the three I already had here with me, I was a mother to that unborn child. Could we afford another baby? During my last pregnancy, I was on complete bed rest from twelve weeks until the birth. Could we afford for me not to work? Having a blended family of seven was a lot, and I had been the sole provider. Could we make it one more and survive? I thought we could make it work. To me, financially it was an issue, but not one that would lead me to make the extreme decision to abort my baby. The pondering finally became too much, so after a few hours I went to tell my predator we were pregnant.

When I told my predator the news, he was shocked and immediately reminded me that this pregnancy was not an option. He was firmly in the mindset that we must do whatever the doctors told us to do. My predator didn't seem to care that him coming inside me would be a big deal. We both knew what the doctors were going to say and I did not want to hear it. My last pregnancy consisted of not being able to eat for five months, a baby who threatened to miscarry (or be born pre-term), as I had a tear in the placenta, and my hips had separated and left me in such pain that I was stuck in a wheelchair, with minimal walking. My body, as the doctors had put it, "was just not made to carry a child." Although I had done it three times before, each pregnancy was extremely tough and each one more worrisome for both baby and myself.

I booked an appointment with the doctor for January 7, 2016. It was the first meeting, where one usually goes to confirm that they are pregnant—a meeting that should have been full of paperwork to have blood work done and discussion of family history. Instead, the doctor said the words I had been dreading: "You cannot do this again. The best option is for you to abort this baby." I asked if there was any chance that we could do a D and C (Dilation and Curettage procedure). My doctor informed me that hospitals no longer do those, and that my only option was to book an appointment with an abortion clinic. I was so beyond frustrated! Why, if I am being told by this doctor that I could not carry this child, could they not do a D and C? That way I could be under anesthetic during the whole thing. Why would they send me to a place where I would have to endure being awake, laying there listening to their machines sucking out my baby, killing him or her? This was beyond imaginable and extremely terrifying. It was not even a choice. I saw ten different doctors, all of whom dealt with pregnancies. All of these doctors had known me during my past pregnancies and knew what I had endured. All ten doctors gave me one option and one option only. "This baby will either kill you both or die on its own. You cannot carry another child. You have to have an abortion." These words broke my heart. They broke me. For another month, while waiting for this unfathomable appointment (with the abortion clinic) that was now booked for February 8th, I again pondered, trying to think of ways that I could do this and not kill either of us. Maybe the doctors were wrong! I ended up becoming ill. So ill, in fact, that I ended up in the hospital on several occasions, being rehydrated and pumped full of meds to help me stop throwing up and having diarrhea every single day. The vomiting became so bad that I began throwing up blood. Panic set in—what was wrong with me? What was happening to my body to cause me to be so sick? What caused the illness to take twenty pounds off my body in only one month? Could the doctors have been right all along? Was this baby going to take my life with its own? How was I to choose my own life over that of my unborn baby? How does anyone make the heart-wrenching decision to end a life, a life that is not their own? I struggled with these thoughts every day.

Now, before I go into the rest of this story, you are probably wondering, what about birth control? Had the method we'd used failed? When I first tried birth control I had major reactions to every type that I had tried, and it was a variety. I had debilitating migraines that did not allow me to work. I ended up getting growths on my ovaries, and I had to have surgery to remove them. I am also allergic to latex, so condoms are not an option—even the latex-free condoms gave me hives. As for other options, I guess not having sex at all would have been a good one. Or my predator, who was going to have a vasectomy and didn't—this would have been another good option. The problem, as it turned out, was that he was a huge procrastinator and huge on sex, and this was one of the reasons that we were in this position.

February 8th, 2016. The day was finally here. I was working my night shift. I was crying through most of it, knowing that soon I was going to allow the doctors to kill my baby. I finished my night shift at 7 a.m. and went home to get ready for what would be a life-altering moment. I was still unsure that I wanted it to happen. My predator, who fully agreed with the doctors, made sure that I made it to my appointment. It was a very quiet ride to the clinic. I had so much running through my head. Perhaps he did, too. My predator was there to support me in every way he could, but there was just one way that he could not. He could not take the pain, anger, or the tears. He couldn't change the hatred I felt for all those who were about to be involved in killing our baby. This included him and myself. The guilt I had over the feelings I was having was unbearable.

We waited in the waiting room for what seemed like forever. I watched and was shocked to see so many other women there to do the same thing I was going to do. I am sure all of them had their own reasons, just as I had. Watching person after person come and go, half an hour passed. There was a psychologist who came out and called my name. The psychologist said it was mandatory to talk to them first to ask if this is what I wanted. My thought was, *No this isn't what I want, this is what I am being told I have to do and there is no other option!*

"How do you feel about what you're about to do?" the psychologist asked. "Like I am about to kill my baby, and that I will die from the guilt that will be with me forever after letting you kill my unborn child." I was beyond angry! I yelled and I screamed and I cried at this person who was a stranger to me, who was only there to help me, to help answer questions and to guide me after this ungodly procedure. The psychologist did not want to allow me to have the procedure that day. She said that I should go home and think about it some more. I was incredulous. How the hell was I to go home, and think about allowing someone to kill my baby, yet have to come back later and say, "Yes, I am good now. I am okay with it. Take my baby and kill it!" It was so extremely frustrating to have to repeat myself, when I just wanted to curl up and die. After she had talked to me, she asked me if I would like anything to remember the baby by. I told her I would like a picture of the baby.

After the Ultrasound was over and they took an image of the baby, they gave me an Ativan and told me to go back and wait in the waiting room. There was so much waiting. After another fifteen minutes of letting the Ativan calm me down, the psychologist came back to get us so she could talk to us both before the procedure. Again she asked if this is what we wanted. My predator informed her once again that this was not a choice, and that we had to do it because of my health. I told her I no longer wanted to talk. Actually, I screamed it at her. I screamed, "I don't want to be here! I don't want to do this! This is how it has to be so no more talking!" She stopped. I cried uncontrollably. I couldn't stop. She left the room for a few minutes to let us talk. He calmly reminded me once more that we were doing this for my health. I said I didn't care. I still didn't want to do this. Then we sat there in silence while I cried. When the psychologist came back into the room, it was time—time to get prepared to have my baby ripped out of me. I sobbed uncontrollably.

The nurse gave me a fuzzy blanket to wrap around my waist. After I changed, I had to sit in a different area and wait for my name to be called while my predator went back to the waiting room. They would call him back into the procedure room when my turn was up. My mom was calling me over and over again. Up to this point no one but my friend knew what was going on. Not even my employers. I had told my work colleagues that I was having surgery on my ovaries. I could not answer my mother's calls. The thoughts that ran through my head, *what would my mother think, first of me being pregnant again and second, of having to abort my baby*, shamed me.

I couldn't talk to her on the phone without crying, so I finally texted her. I told her that I would not be able to call and talk to her for a few days. I told her that we found out we were pregnant in December, right after Christmas. I told her what we were about to do. I told her that I was about to let these doctors kill my baby. I don't know how I managed to write to her through the flood of tears, but I did. My mom, being supportive, said that it was the right choice and that I couldn't be pregnant again and survive. She told me she loved me and that this was the most unselfish thing I could do and that, when I was ready, I could talk to her. Then I cried so hard because I don't like to lie to my family, and I had been hiding the situation from them for a month. I had told them that I had a bad flu when I was super-sick and in and out of the hospital. In fact, they did not know that I had to go to the hospital on more than one occasion. I felt like the worst person ever.

It was time. My heart was beating so fast as they called my name. I was shaking and couldn't stop. The tears just flowed. I couldn't look at anyone. I couldn't talk. We walked into the room where the procedure was about to take place and they told me to climb up onto the table. I had to put my legs hanging over these supports that kept them spread open. The nurse was talking to me, and I could only muster up the sounds, "uh huh." She was trying to give me an IV, but she missed. She said, "Well, at least you have lots of other good veins." She was trying to lighten the mood. I thought, seriously, I am not here because you need someone with good veins! I am here because I was left with no choice. She stuck me again and got the IV to adminis-ter the medicine that was supposed to help with the pain and to help keep me calm. They said I should not remember most of this.

They were so very wrong! I remember it all. I lay there and looked at the ceiling while the doctor came in. The ceiling had a picture of a fairy flying. It was a beautiful painting. I tried to focus on that. The doctor checked to see where my cervix was and explained what she was about to do. She first stuck needles in to freeze around the cervix... it was supposed to help with the pain. It didn't. As the suctioning started, I could feel the pain of the needle. It hurt badly. I cried out in pain. Mental pain because I was losing my baby at that moment, and because the physical pain was unbearable. I wanted to shout, "Stop!" but I knew that it was too late. The nurse said she would give me more pain killers. But they didn't work. The pain was now imprinted on my memory, something I will never forget. Throughout the procedure, my predator was there to hold my hand for comfort and support... I could not even look at him. I looked at the painting on the ceiling; I looked in the opposite direction. I didn't want him to see me weak and crying. When the doctor completed the procedure, her exact words were, "We are all done and we got it all." I was angry at these words. You just killed my baby and you nonchalantly just said all done? I couldn't take any more.

After the procedure, they had me walk to another room with my predator. They gave me ibuprofen for the pain and cramping. There was very little bleeding. We went home about fifteen minutes after the procedure. I couldn't talk to my predator; I couldn't even look at him the whole ride home. I was angry with him. When we arrived home I went straight to bed. I cried and cried. I went over the procedure in my head. I felt as though I had made a huge mistake. How I should have, somehow, saved this tiny being, and that I didn't do my job as a mother to protect him or her. I had two days to "get over this loss" before having to go back to work. I barely came out of the room and when I did, I didn't speak. I didn't want to talk, but my brain wouldn't shut off, going over and over again what I had just done.

When I finally fell asleep, the nightmares came right away. In my dreams, I was very sore from the procedure, and my predator had taken the baby to the car and came back and got me. As we walked to the car, I could hear my baby screaming in pain! I panicked and ran to the car to see what was wrong. As I approached the car there was a person in the front driver seat. I opened the door and asked, "What are you doing to my baby?!" I then pulled them out of the car. As I pulled him out, I could see my baby stuck in between the front seat and the door frame screaming. I looked at the person I had pulled out of the vehicle and asked, "Why?" and then I was suddenly stabbing them. As they slowly looked up at me, I saw the face of the person I was stabbing. It was the face of a baby. I awoke crying and shaking.

I had another dream of my baby dying in a tornado. Every dream I had, I tried to save my baby. Every dream I had, the baby died. Every time, when I woke, I cried from all the guilt and sadness of how horrible I was for not being the best mom possible, and instead allowing a doctor to take a needle and kill my little defenseless baby.

Having to work two days after losing my baby, with little sleep and a whole lot on my mind was not easy—another thing that my predator failed to think of when he accidentally came inside me for his own pleasure. Friends I had made at work were pregnant and almost due to have their babies. It was hard to pretend I was okay, and not be able to talk about what had really happened. On my first shift back, about midway, the thoughts became so unbearable that I considered taking the knife I used to cut boxes open with to slice my wrists, while at the same time trying to figure out a way to make it look like an accident. I do not know what stopped me at that moment. Maybe someone walked by and called my name. I don't remember but I am grateful. I had these thoughts on more than one occasion.

On my second shift back, I began having severe pain in my pelvis. So much so that I could barely walk. I left early to go back to see a doctor. I called the abortion clinic, since they ask you to go back to them if you have any problems after the procedure. I dreaded having to go back to the very place where my baby was killed. I was given an appointment for 9:30. When I arrived I couldn't even sit in a chair the pain was so bad. When the nurse called my name, I could hardly even walk towards her. She said, "I can see the pain all over your face." The doctor came into the room and did an exam. She said that she couldn't see anything wrong, but she prescribed antibiotics anyway. The doctor then said that if the pain persisted after the medication was finished I should call them back.

The antibiotics lasted seven days and at the end of those seven days the pain was worse! I called the clinic back again. The nurse said she would talk to the doctor and call me back. I awaited her call back. When she did call me back she informed me that they were done with me now, and that if I was still in pain then it must be from something else and not from them doing the procedure. Basically she dismissed me. I was angry! I was crying because the pain was so bad. I was crying because I let them take my baby and I was in serious pain from the procedure they had done. I cried because if I hadn't let them do this, none of this would be happening. People tell me I did the most unselfish thing I could do. Did I really? Was killing an innocent baby being unselfish? I felt like I had this huge hole in me. In my heart, in my stomach... I didn't want to cry anymore. I felt like I didn't deserve the right to do that. I didn't eat a lot as I felt that was the only control over myself I had. It was day by day, and there was no control. I would either not cry and feel dead inside, or I would cry in silence and wish I could stop. Every day I was reminded that I would never have my baby to hold and protect! What I was supposed to do... Protect my child. I failed. What kind of mother kills their child? One who hasn't even taken a breath outside the womb?

My predator told me I had to get rid of my baby. Told me I had to for my health. He didn't seem to care that afterwards I would still have the responsibilities to look after all the bills, the kids, and the household chores, while working seventeen hours a day. My predator lost his job on February 9, 2016. His boss made it clear to him (so my predator told me) that they could see he no longer had an interest to work there. They told him to either take a demotion or leave. He left. Now I lost my baby, and I also had to make up what was not coming into the home. It was so much stress. So much anxiety.

Continuing to work seventeen hours a day and not sleeping because of reoccurring nightmares of the baby led to Post Traumatic Stress Disorder. My body physically began to crumble. Doctors' orders were to cut back on nights and eventually never work nights again. All I could think was now what? I need this job. I need this money. A posting came up at work in May of 2016. Things at work were taking a drastic turn and anyone could apply for management. I had started working someday shifts along with evenings before applying to become management. I worked hard and I worked fast. I was an asset to this team. This is the promotion that my predator became angry about because it was causing longer than normal shifts. I wanted to be an assistant manager. One job. One salary. I was excited! For the first time in the year since the loss, I was excited. I wanted to move up the ladder. It had promise and hope.

My predator began to make me feel guilty. I was still working seventeen-hour days. I just did it all in a row with no break. My break was to sleep and then do it again the next day. I began taking overtime shifts. I wanted the experience. My predator started coming to my work with my son to "get out" to "say Hi." When I got home he continually asked who I talked too, who I drove home (as I worked evenings I drove a couple of people home on my way so they wouldn't have to take a bus at midnight), and what took me so long. My response was short. Good night I am going to bed. My predator would follow me into the bedroom. Nightly he tucked me in, but not without trying to rub me down first. I had started going to bed fully clothed after my son was born in 2014. After the loss of my baby in 2016, I had a huge drop in sexual drive. That, however, didn't stop my predator from continuing to pressure me for sex, and some days succeeding because I was so tired of trying to fight him off—I just let him do it.

Even after the loss of the baby my predator refused to help keep me protected from another pregnancy and used the pull-out method. He showed no concern for what I had gone through. He tried to hold me. Tried to get me to eat, but also never stopped trying to get into my pants. Never stopped having his hand to his crotch while laying beside me in bed. Trying to reach my arm and guide it back behind me so I could help him get off. He didn't care that my arm snapped from the awkward angle that he was dragging it into. I kept motionless. Not moving sometimes made it stop. Remembering to breathe quietly and not with panic so that he didn't think I was awake and continue his efforts to have intercourse. My predator never gave up. I feel like there was shift in me. A shift to start pushing back. I told him he was waking me. He was being rough. I told my predator that he needed to stop. My predator told me that he was doing these things in his sleep. I found this odd because he started as soon as he crawled into bed. Coming over and rubbing circles around my crotch, trying to spread my butt cheeks so he could slide his penis in between and rub. It wasn't always nightly. It started with once or twice a week.

I am sure that my not being in the mood made him crave sex even more. "Any physical contact would be better than none to feel closer to you," he said. My focus began to change. I was beginning to remember who I had wanted to be. I was fighting for that person. In July 2016, I was promoted! I worked my ass off. I rarely needed guidance and had the smarts to get others to get things done. Management noticed this and started to prep me for assistant management. Even more exciting! I loved my job. My predator was okay with the promotion but didn't like me working late at night. Some nights I would get the silent treatment. I would get, "you never messaged me today while you were at work." I would tell him I was busy, because I was, in fact, busy. Nothing satisfied him anymore. I started to notice more subtle changes in his behaviour. He was becoming more obsessive, more possessive... more paranoid. I wasn't overly concerned at the time—it was gradual enough so that I didn't think, *Wow! What the hell is going on with you?*—but it did make me think.

Chapter Four

ILLNESS

BEING RUN DOWN does so many horrible things to one's body. Everything can become out of whack. For me, it was building up over time, and it finally made its presence known on August 26, 2017, after being misdiagnosed for two weeks with pleurisy. I was told to take time off of work—work that I needed to help my family stay afloat. I didn't know that being misdiagnosed would have such a profound impact on my life. I went into the emergency room with severe pain in the right upper quadrant of my stomach just under the ribs. This pain was so unbearable that my skin looked grey and my lips were blue because the pain prevented me from being able to take normal breaths.

On Sept 12, 2017, I was diagnosed with gallstones, and I needed my gallbladder to be removed the very next day. I was told of possible complications like bleeding and snipping wrong arteries, but nowhere did it say there is a 1/1,000,000 chance I would get a rare complication. Seemed like good odds. The complications started with simple pain, and the pain while eating, over time, would become so bad I would throw up. The pain was intolerable, and I spent many days going back and forth to the hospital so the doctors could try and figure out what was going on. I could barely stand up; I was often curled up in a ball because the pain radiated from my stomach to my back and up through my shoulder blades.

They did multiple tests, including cat scans, MRIs, painful ultrasounds, HIDA scans, blood work, blood cultures, and a gastronomy, and there was still no indication as to what was causing the problem. The only thing that popped up every so often on my blood work was liver enzyme increases. This signified needing an endoscopic retrograde cholangio-pancreatography (ERCP) to correct a little muscle called the Sphincter of Oddi, a tiny little rubber band-like thing that had closed off and was preventing the pancreatic juices and liver enzymes from properly breaking down my food, causing extreme pain. The downside to this procedure was the chance of complications—there was twenty-five percent chance the procedure would cause pancreatitis.

The procedure caused the most severe pain I have ever been in. It was so bad I couldn't breathe. Even Fentanyl didn't work. Every move made me sick. My doctor knew right away I had moderately severe acute pancreatitis. The way to correct it and allow it to heal is to stop all food and drink from going through the stomach. One week later, and I still had unfathomable pain. I was still throwing up, and woke soaked in sweat as the pain meds wore off. I remember waking and crying out to the nurse to just help me get to the shower. I thought the hot water would help. It was then decided I would need a nasojejunal tube (NJ) to get some nutrients. They had to start slow with the feeding tube. Too fast or too much at first meant puking it all up. Forty-six days in the hospital, and I was poked daily to have blood work done, poked daily to have my IV put back in as my body seemed to reject them, and of course, the bedtime needle for the nightly blood clots. Eventually, there was only a couple of nurses who would touch me to reinsert the IV. No one else was brave enough.

My predator came to visit nightly, but I noticed a change in his behaviour and mannerism. He kept asking me who came to visit me, and when I said, "no one," he kept pushing saying, "no one came to see you at all?" I said, "No, no one has been coming because I am not strong enough to keep up a conversation—the pain meds make me sleepy." I told him he could ask the nurse, as my bed was right across from the nurses' desk. He didn't seem happy with those answers. I did have a couple of visitors, though. Three of my girlfriends came, and my ex-husband, who kept my two older boys, brought them to the hospital every weekend to see me.

My predator was aware that these visitors were coming. His change in mood made me use his long work day as an excuse to try to keep him from visiting. I told him it was okay if he couldn't come if he was tired. When he thought he was getting sick, I told him to stay home so that he didn't give it to me, and make me even sicker. Regardless of what I said, he showed up most evenings. Even when he was at home, he managed to keep harassing me about sex. Again starting with nude selfies, to cum shots, and then to porn pictures of people masturbating in a group, and even sending me a video of him coming. He also sent me nudes of him wearing my thongs and underwear to work telling me my underwear was so comfortable and sent another video of him coming in my underwear. His pushy behaviour never stopped; it worsened. I was scared. I could feel myself start to pull away.

I was released from the hospital on Mar 3, 2018. I was terrified to go home—I didn't feel strong enough. The doctor had just pulled out the NJ tube for the second time before I was released. Nasty taste, but could have been worse. I went home on a diet that was no more than three hundred calories, as this is how small my stomach had become after forty-six days. When I went home, my body was completely deconditioned. When I walked, my body vibrated. When I talked, I had a hard time concentrating on multiple people talking at once, or with what I was trying to say. My balance was really off. Noise, any noise, sounded amplified by ten times. My heart raced—my heart rate was in the 170s—and my blood pressure was higher. I was so weakened.

I ended up back in Emergency on Mar 5th. I was hospitalized again because I couldn't keep any food in my body. I couldn't even walk from my bathroom to my bed in the hospital without assistance. My doctor ran more tests, but everything came back okay. He asked me why I didn't want to go home, and told me he was going to get a psychologist to come talk to me. I sat there and cried; one, because the pain was unbearable; two, because I was so weak, and I didn't understand how they could send me home in a state where I could not function without help; and three, because I was scared. I was scared because of my illness, because I almost died, and because of my predator's worsening behaviour.

The psychologist came into the room, and started asking me questions—asking me why I didn't want to go home. I didn't know it at the time, but it was because I feared my predator. I feared being alone with him. I feared not being able to push him off. I feared being trapped. By this point, while I was at the hospital my predator said his vehicle wasn't running properly and needed work and was now using my vehicle, even when I was home from the hospital he took over the use of my vehicle, and he had taken my debit card, and spent my money freely. I was careful while in the hospital. I put only small amounts of money on the card at a time, telling him we didn't have any to waste. After speaking with my psychologist, I confronted my predator. I told him that he needed to change. I told him he needed to step up or we weren't going to make it. I think this is where I went wrong. I remember the look he gave me as, "how dare you!" This was my first time really pushing back and challenging my predator. I was terrified.

On March 9th, I was released from the hospital again. Still able to take in only three hundred calories a day, I was extremely weak, shaky, and fatigued. My heart raced. It didn't take long before things got more worrisome. My predator started asking me more and more who I was talking to all day, he wanted to know who I was messaging while he was at work, and who had been in our home while he was away. I had nothing to hide, and I offered him my phone. He said he didn't need to see it, but I felt like I was being accused of things that were just not happening, so I took a screen shot of every conversation and sent it to him. I told him he needed to stop assuming stuff.

My three-year old son had been staying with my sister in Calgary while I was in the hospital and recovering. Daily, I FaceTime'd with my son, sometimes even from bed. I would open the curtain so that my son could see my face. Prior to getting ill, I rarely opened the curtains. My predator came home and asked, who came over? He asked me why the curtains open? He said that his ex-wife used to open the curtains when she cheated on him. I assured him that it was only to allow our son to see my face. He came home daily, mid-shift from work, to see what I was doing. I learned to lock the door when I was in the bath, which pissed him off.

My predator's paranoia worsened. He told me he was watching my "toy" to see if I was using it. Again, I reassured him that this was something I was not ready for, as my body hurt. Everything hurt. His obsession was scary—I would catch him or hear him going through all my drawers, my closet, my belongings. *What was he looking for*, I wondered? I was becoming terrified of what was to come next. I just wonder who else finds this as creepy as I did. I felt a major evasion of privacy, and I felt dirty.

Chapter Five

THE ESCALATION

ON MARCH 22, 2018, I got a message from my predator while he was at work saying, "I am sorry if me laying next to you at night wakes you..." All I could think was, *he can't be this clueless.* I was angry with him. Every single day since getting out of the hospital I had been pressured by touch, pictures, and actions of a sexual nature.

My predator seemed to have no boundaries, so again, on a weekend in March after his message, I told him that he needed to stop pressuring me—to stop sending me messages with naked pictures, to stop touching me inappropriately at night, and waking me roughly. I told him that his paranoia was going to end us. Again he said the words "I am sorry." "Sorry" was becoming a blank word with no meaning. Nothing ever changed.

I was extremely careful not to lead my predator on. I was cautious about sitting near him because he stated once, "I can't help if sitting next to you turns me on." I was cautious not to lead him on by kissing him passionately. I talked to friends about what was happening at night; I was becoming more vocal about being groped and grabbed and hurt at night by him. I literally went to bed scared and dreading the sound of our bedroom door opening, knowing that as soon as he came to bed, he was coming for me. I asked for any advice I could get to see how to end this. The advice I got from that mutual friend of ours was, "If I were you and it was that bad, I would go sleep on the couch." So I tried that. My predator angrily told me to get back to bed.

Another friend, who was a male, told me to try watching him get off. Perhaps that's all he needed to relax. So I tried that in October of 2017. It didn't work. It made him more horny. It caused more pressure to do the "deed." It was getting so bad that I dreaded getting dressed in front of him. I was completely uncomfortable with him even being in the room.

I finally got up the courage to ask my mom what she would do. I didn't sound panicked or scared. My mom didn't get any clues from me that something was really wrong. I started talking to more people about it, asking my doctor about it, and if my predator's behaviour was normal. He assured me it was not.

On April 22, 2018, something happened that I was not expecting. I went for a shower, something I did super-carefully and hurriedly, as every time I came out of the shower, my predator was waiting for me in our bedroom lying fully naked and exposed, anticipating me dropping my towel to get dressed, while he would masturbate. At other times he would follow me into the bedroom after I got out of the shower, dried off, and went into our bedroom to get dressed—this was still just as awkward, still with an uneasy feeling, as he would casually remove my towel, and then his clothes, to try and initiate sex.

This day was no different. I hurriedly went from the bathroom to my bedroom carefully listening for the sound of the back door, as I heard my predator leave to go to the garage for a smoke. I failed to hear him come back in because I was on the phone, sitting on the corner of the bed, already dressed. My predator came into the room just as I was finishing up my call. He closed the door behind him. My eyes widened with nervousness.

My predator slowly came over and pushed me backwards onto the bed, laying me down. He then tried repeatedly to remove my pants. I was not giving up so fast; I fought. I held on to my pants as he tried to pull them down. I told him, NO! My predator climbed off me. Got up and locked the bedroom door. He then came back to the bed and had to reposition me back on the bed because when he got up, so did I.

My predator tried to remove my pants again. This time I shouted hoping the kids would hear me from downstairs, at the very least his fifteen-year-old son. I shouted, "what part of fucking NO don't you understand," and tried to push him away with my feet. My predator smiled. He told me that he just wanted to lick me. I froze. My predator for the second time climbed off me. He stood before me and removed his clothing. I was halfway laying down unsure what to expect next and halfway from sitting up on the bed. My predator then got on the bed beside me, laid down and started to slowly rub his penis up and down. I sat straight up. Too scared to leave the room. My predator asked me if I wanted to touch him. I was quick to reply, "NO."

My predator finished himself off and as soon as he was done I quickly left the room. I was unsure of what had just happened, but I knew I was scared. He tried to hug me, and I pushed him away. He gave me an awkward smirk. My kids needed to be fed. It was Sunday, late afternoon, and they had school the next day. All I could think was, *What just happened? What's going to happen?* I gave my predator the benefit of the doubt, thinking his actions were out of frustration for the lack of intimacy over the last several months.

April 23, 2018, my predator texted me telling me that if he had to sit in the house one more night alone he would put a gun to his head. This text came while he was at work. I knew my illness was taking a toll. I was always really tired while trying to heal. I always tried to go to bed around eight.

I told my predator that we needed groceries and perhaps we could do that together. He said okay after I convinced him that I wanted him to come. That evening after he was done work we went shopping. It took about an hour and a half. We were home before 8 p.m. While shopping, my predator and I talked about watching a movie. I thought I would make the effort to try to stay up. When we got home, my predator unpacked the groceries, and then went out for a smoke in the garage. When he came back in, he told me he was going for a shower.

I thought we were going to watch a movie. I sat on the couch wondering what was to come. This night it was only the two of us in the house. No kids. After his shower he went into the bedroom. He was in there for a bit. I didn't move off the couch. I continued to look on Facebook marketplace for a new bed for my stepdaughter, a new big-girl bed. My predator came out of the room with only pants on. He didn't sit down. He walked over to the back patio door through the kitchen and locked it up, and then through the living room to tell me he was going to bed.

I was stunned. All this time I thought he wanted to just spend time together, even if it was just a movie. I said, "Okay. Goodnight." I stayed on the couch, and continued to look for a new bed. I didn't move. I was there for about an hour after my predator went to bed. I was hoping he would fall asleep before me, thinking he wouldn't wake me that night, but he came out twice in that hour, asking me when I was coming to bed. My heart pounded. I still had zero strength.

About 9 p.m. and after the second time my predator came out and asked me when I was coming to bed, I figured I should try to get some sleep. I had a doctor's appointment the next day, and I needed to rest. I got up from the couch and walked slowly to the bathroom, which was right beside my bedroom. I noticed the bedroom light was on through the space at the bottom of the door. My stomach sank. I continued on into the bathroom to do my nightly routine. Once finished, I stalled at the bedroom door, scared of what was awaiting the other side.

Just as I had dreaded, my predator was laying naked and fully exposed. I turned out the light before making my way around to my side of the bed. I took my medication for pain and sleep, and I didn't bother to remove any of the clothing I wore that day. I crawled into bed facing him. My predator immediately started kissing me. Trying to passionately kiss me and I moved back. At one point I even tried to move my cheek to his mouth to show I was not interested.

My predator started with the same routine that he had tried just the day before. He tried to remove my pants over and over and over again while I laid there so angry, so frustrated that this was happening. I again held on to my pants, not giving into his persistent way. Fifteen long minutes went by. I had pillows between us and I even tried to roll away from him hoping that he would get a clue—I am not in the mood to be touched yet again.

Nope. He continued. I got so scared and so frustrated—I just wanted him to stop. He didn't. He then stuck his hands down my pants grabbing my crotch and tried to insert his finger into my vagina. I clamped my legs closed as hard as I could. He then moved his hand to my backside inside my pants, circling my bum with his finger. His hand finally slowly came out and I thought, *Okay, he's done. I can breathe.* I felt like I had been holding my breath forever; I hoped he was giving up.

He didn't stop. He kept trying to remove my pants kissing my neck, kissing my cheek, kissing my shoulder. My brain was on fire, searching for answers on how to make it stop. I just wanted it to stop. I gave in, thinking if I just give him head he will leave my body alone. So impatiently, I turned over to face my predator sprawled back onto the bed. I started to suck his penis. Holding back the tears and praying he would stop. He didn't stop. His hands made it around me to my pants again, and again he tried to take them off. This time it was harder to fight to keep them up. I got so frustrated and scared because he was not stopping, and I felt the only way to make this stop was to give in. I got up roughly and pissy and took my own pants off. I continued oral on him hoping to make him come as fast as I could. In the meantime he managed to stick his middle finger inside me and start thrusting it in and out while trying to do oral on me as well. For a split second he stopped and asked me if it hurt. I said, "Yes it hurts, but I suppose I should get over it, right?" He continued. My predator thought that I should overcome my pain, the fear of the pain I would have by having sex, as it was still painful all over my body. I finally made him come. I jumped off the bed and got dressed as fast as I could. Usually I would go pee again but I was frozen with fear. Fear that if I left the room he would follow me. Fear if I stayed much worse would happen. I curled up around my pillows and pulled the blankets in close and closed my eyes to let the tears fall silently onto my pillow. I didn't sleep that night. I couldn't. I feared that I would be awakened in the middle of the night to a much worse sexual assault.

That's what it was... **Sexual Assault**.

The next day, I had a doctor's appointment later on that afternoon. I told my predator I needed my vehicle that day. My predator told me he would come with me to the doctor. I told him I needed to go alone. I also told my predator that I would be going to visit a friend after my appointment. I actually left the house in the morning. I was too scared to stick around.

My predator kept messaging me, telling me we needed to talk, that he knew I was mad about the night before, but that he was sorry. My predator told me I was breaking his heart. *I was breaking his heart?!* I couldn't stop crying.

I went to see my friend at work to tell her what happened. I stayed with her for a bit while she tried to comfort me. I finally had to go to my doctor's appointment. I told my doctor about the past two days' events and asked him to document it in my file. He did so. What he didn't tell me was that I could go and have a rape kit done. Saliva will stay in and on your body for up to seven days, and can be tested. Seven days. I am not sure my doctor knew this information or thought at the time maybe that I would need it. I had no clue until it was too late.

After my doctor's appointment, I went to my friend's house. I knew I was safe there because my predator didn't know where she lived. I stayed with her for a few hours. While there, I also messaged my friend from down east and told her what had happened. Next, my sister called. My friend from down east told her what had happened. My sister told me I needed to get out of there.

I agreed, but having no strength, I was scared. I was scared that if I didn't go home that night, my predator would not go into work the following day, and would wait for me. He was messaging me constantly while I was at my friend's house. He asked when I would be home, begged me not to leave him, told me he was sorry, that we needed to talk. Told me he promised not to touch me. I went home that night after visiting my kids at my ex-husband's house. I needed their hugs, and I needed to stall. While I was with my kids, I received many calls and many messages from my predator. They were getting angrier. "It's 9 at night, and you should be home." I told him I was coming home, but I would not be sleeping in our room. I told him I didn't want to talk. He said, "You have the bedroom; I will sleep downstairs."

When I got home around 11 p.m., he was waiting for me. I didn't say Hi. I went straight to the bathroom to get ready for bed. He followed me into the bedroom. He begged me not to leave him. Told me he would never touch me again. I told him I was tired and needed to sleep. He gave me a hug and kiss on the cheek and left the room.

Wednesday, April 25, 2018. Another day I didn't feel safe to be home. I stayed home for most of the day, but I planned to leave that evening before my predator returned home from work. My kids had a school function that evening, giving me the perfect excuse to not be home. I received messages all day long, asking me why I didn't want him to come to the kids' function at school. This is something I had asked him to do many times before, but he never came. I told him it would be awkward since I was not talking to him right now, and it was the kid's night; I didn't want to ruin it. I told him that I would not be coming straight home afterwards; I would be going to another friend's house.

My predator came home around 11:30 a.m. that day. He came to "check on me." I timed it so that I was in the bath. I locked the bathroom door so he could not come in. He was mad, yelling, "Really?!" I waited until he left, when I could hear the back door on the patio open, close, and lock before getting out of the tub. I wanted to make sure he was gone. My predator messaged me telling me he would be home earlier than usual. I panicked. I told him I was leaving early. I had no reason to, other than because I did not want to be in the house alone with him. I sat in my car. I parked it near my kid's daycare, a place I knew he wouldn't look to find me. I then received these messages from him:

"You're breaking my heart right now. You know that, right?"

"Am I that bad a person that you can't even say hi to me on the phone?"

"You don't want to talk to me, then ok. But this isn't helping anything. You're making me feel alienated. Like you're trying to distance yourself so it's easier to pull away. You've never been on this side before. Please don't run from me."

I was completely stunned. I didn't understand how he could think that me being angry was not a normal reaction. So I responded to these messages including every single thing he and I had discussed within the last several months. Here is what I said:

"Your heart's not the only one breaking. Mine is broken. You were the one person I should have been able to trust and feel safe with. In a two-day span, you managed to break my trust and physically hurt me. So, yes, I may be pulling back. I need time. Time to think. Time to understand what made you think it was okay. There is so much about what you have been doing that is wrong.

The other stuff, bills, and house, and all that other crap, I felt maybe things could change, and one day be better. But with you acting the way you have, I don't know. You're paranoid, you've compared me to your ex and how she used to cheat on you; you constantly ask who I am talking to or messaging. You say you have nothing to live for if I leave... so what does that mean... your kids mean nothing? You say you're not yourself. I feel you're not the same person I fell in love with. I don't know what changed.

I am not sure how to fix this. I just know right now you have made me feel uncomfortable to be home or to be near you."

I was so unbelievably mad. How dare you tell me your heart is broken! How dare you! I never thought I would fall victim to abuse. At this point, I still didn't even know that what he was doing to me was abuse. Of course he could not help himself and had to respond to my message.

"Ok. When I say I would have nothing to live for I mean that would be the end of any love life for me. I love my kids and would never do anything to hurt them."

"I do trust you. This was my issue, which I made yours, and I told you I'm making that better. I didn't compare you to my ex-wife. There is no comparison. You are a great woman and I really want to show you that, if you give me the chance. It's your body, yours alone.

"I know what I did was wrong. It won't happen again. I promise you that. And by me not being myself and totally focused on you, especially since you've been sick. I am changing that as well.

"I know you won't feel better about it overnight, understandable. But I would love it if you would give me another chance, to be the man you fell in love with, the father our kids need, and person I want to be. Just let me prove to you that this is where we belong. I can't say enough to express how bad I feel, and I never wanted to hurt you. Please let me help mend your broken heart and keep our family together. I love you always."

I never responded to this message. I went to my kids' school function and then went to my friend's house. While I was at my friend's, I received many text messages and eight phone calls within less than a ten-minute span, all of which I chose not to answer. My friend watched these calls come in, and said, "That is scary behaviour." He was right.

I was scared to go home, but again, I feared not going because he would stay home from work the next day. I went home around 9:30 p.m. When I did get home, my predator was waiting for me again. This time he was waiting in the kitchen for me. I slowly took my boots off. I slowly went into the kitchen to get my bedtime medication and had a sip of water. Then I proceeded to walk right past him, but he grabbed my wrists and slumped backwards into the kitchen cabinets. Again telling me how sorry he was. How much he loved me; he begged me not to leave him. I tried to pull away, but he hung on and pulled me back roughly. I told him I wanted to go to bed. He held on a second longer, and then released me. I went to the bathroom, did my nightly routine and went to bed, where yet again, my predator followed me. He pecked my cheek, gave me a hug, and said, "Please don't leave me. I love you." Then he left the bedroom.

Chapter Six

THE DAY I LEFT

ON APRIL 26, 2018, at around ten in the morning I brought my vehicle into my friend's shop. This friend is one of the people I had been talking to about the nightly waking's, and asking advice on how to make it stop. This day he could see something was wrong.

I didn't start a conversation with him. I sat quietly on the bench after handing him my keys. I needed work on the engine. While sitting there quietly I started to silently sob. My friend came over and asked if I wanted to talk. I told him no so he got up to walk away. But he came back. He asked if everything was okay. I shook my head no. He asked if I felt safe to go home. I shook my head no. He didn't need to hear the details to know I needed help.

That friend immediately got his therapist on the phone to speak with me. His therapist listened to everything I had to tell him. He then told me I needed to get out of my home, because he felt that I was not safe to be there. He told me he felt that if I stayed that things would get worse and escalate. I was so scared. I was shaking so bad. In the midst of all the chaos over the last couple days remembering to nourish my body escaped my brain. Instead I was struggling with another form of survival.

After speaking to my friend's therapist, the therapist asked to speak to my friend. I don't know what he said to him but my friend told me I was not to leave and go home. My friend called his friend who was an ex-police officer. He asked him to come and talk with me and give me options. The ex-officer was very kind. We sat in his truck outside the shop. I was bawling my face off and visibly shaken. He told me if I report it with the police and leave my predator then things could get worse. If I don't report it with the police that I should still leave. He left the choice up to me but also asked me if I wanted to talk to the Sexual Assault Crisis Hotline. My hands were shaking so bad I couldn't even look up the number. My friend let me talk to the ex-officer alone, but then came to check on us. He told the ex-officer, "Look at her shaking. She cannot go home."

My friend and the ex-officer walked me back into the shop. My legs collapsed beneath me. They both grabbed an arm and helped me back in. By this point my mind and body were both totally broken down from exhaustion and pain. The ex-officer gave me the number to the crisis center hotline. I spoke with them, and they explained that I needed to make a plan of escape. If I could not leave that day, I had to pretend like things were okay so things at home did not escalate. I decided right then that if I was going to leave, today would be the day.

My predator was in court with his ex-wife. Today was my chance to leave. I got off the phone and my friend offered me food. I gratefully ate a small banana and drank a little water. My friend asked for my dad's phone number so he could call him and tell him what was happening. He told my dad he would keep me safe. He then handed over the phone.

I cried so hard while trying to explain to my father that the person I trusted assaulted me. Telling my father I was too terrified to go home. My father was calm. He told me what I needed to hear. Permission to leave. Don't get me wrong, I didn't "need" his permission, but I did need to hear the words it was okay to leave. I was feeling guilty as many abused people do, for breaking up my family. For thinking my kids are not going to understand. But my dad, with a few simple words, eased my mind for a bit.

I hung up the phone with my dad. I told him I had to go home and get what I could before my predator returned from court. I only had a small window of time. My friend put me up in a hotel for the night so I could rest before driving down three hours to my family in Calgary. I told my friend I would be back.

I hustled to the bank to grab $200 cash to leave my predator. Why, I don't know; I just thought it would be best. I got home and I still do not know how I managed to run and walk so quickly through my home to gather up my belongings, my kids' belongings, and anything of importance to my children and me. My mom stayed on the phone the whole time. I told her my heart hurt. It was pounding so fast, and I was extremely short of breath, but she said, "Stay on the phone." I did. The last thing I did was throw the $200 on the counter before leaving the house. I locked up and never looked back.

I drove back to my friend's shop to show him I was okay, and to thank him again, but on the way to the shop, my sister called me. She told me that my predator called her, and asked where I was going. I missed my predator coming home by ten minutes. I took a deep breath. I continued to the shop to thank my friend. He gave me the hotel address; he wished me well, and told me to keep in touch.

I took it slow. I was watching every vehicle driving by me. I was so scared he would find me. I received message after message. Call after call and then our mutual friends started to call. I didn't answer any that day except one. I waited till I got to the hotel and felt safe before calling her back. I needed to tell her what happened. She asked if I was safe. I told her yes. I didn't tell her where I was but that I was safe. We chatted a little while and then I wanted to go for a shower. I felt dirty.

After getting out of the shower I had several voicemails from my predator along with text messages and Facebook messages. Asking me where I was, telling me in a voicemail that he would be coming for me in Calgary. I was so scared. Now my family was at risk. I didn't respond to his messages that night. I called my family to reassure them I was safe and then I turned my phone off.

In the morning I collected my thoughts and got my things packed, took a deep breath and dialed my predator's phone number. I told my predator that what he did to me was unforgivable. I told my predator I could no longer trust him. I told my predator that I was scared of him and what else he would do. I told my predator I would not be returning home. My predator became desperate trying to say anything to get me to go back. "I promise to get help," "I love you so much—please don't do this to me," "I will follow you down to Calgary." I was firm and told him that our conversations were limited to talking about our shared son, who was three, and the household items that needed to be split up.

My predator begged and pleaded with me not to do this. He told me that he was sick and needed help. He told me that if I wanted him to get help he would. I told him again that I could not forgive what has been happening, nor do I trust him. I told him, "I am not coming back, and I need to get off the phone now." He said, "Okay. I love you." After hanging up, I got my bags and I headed south towards Calgary.

The days that followed leaving my predator were not any easier. Because we shared a three-year-old son, I felt it was important that we be civil. I was firm to make sure my predator knew our conversations were still limited to only messaging about our son and the household stuff we needed to sort out. Unfortunately, with any sort of contact, keeping it to these two topics was not what he wanted, nor seemed able to comply with.

My predator strayed away on conversations going back and forth from loving to blaming. He didn't seem to understand or grasp I wanted nothing to do with him. Over and over again, I had to remind him to stick to the topics I was willing to talk about. My predator couldn't seem to keep the same focus. At every angle he wanted to talk to me alone, to give him five minutes of my time so he could explain his side of things and why it happened the way it did. To me there was no explanation that was going to allow me to forgive him for his assaults. He asked if he could talk to me on the phone. I told him No, but he could message me about the two topics. He asked me if I just wanted him to message me so that it was all written down. As much as I hadn't really thought about it, it made sense, and boy, am I ever glad I did it that way! Our society is powerful with words. Many of these words are in the form of social media, emails, and of course, text messages.

My predator was getting desperate. Every night telling me he missed me, while FaceTime'ing with our three-year-old son, and telling me he still loves me. I refused to turn the phone on me so he could see me. My family stood behind my choices. Up until this point, I was still debating reporting the assault to the police. I was scared to report it. My dad was scared, too, that if I reported it that it would just make things even worse. I struggled but spoke to a friend at a family law firm, and another friend who works as an RCMP officer, to ask what advice they could give me. Both said I should report it.

On May 6, 2018, my predator sent me over three hundred text messages and Facebook private messages. My mom and I stood there, in awe of his continuous harassment. In forty-five minutes he sent one hundred and ten messages. I told my mom I was scared. He wasn't stopping. Every day, from the time I left till May 7, 2018, he continued to message me unwanted messages. My mom messaged him to stop. Here are just a few of the messages that he sent.

May 6, 2018, starting at 3:12 p.m.:

> "I was trying to keep the house, but that is not viable now
>
> So I'll be moving out as well
>
> I don't know where considering I'll have less money than you
>
> But somewhere
>
> Don't think for one minute I don't hold myself accountable for stuff
>
> But we both made mistakes
>
> Read what I texted you
>
> You'll see I get it
>
> I'm going to let you go
>
> I won't stop loving you but I will let you go
>
> Because that's what YOU want
>
> You will never have to fear me
>
> Get better
>
> And move on

I'll be happy in my life

But I won't love another. I told you that and I meant it

You were it for me

I think you still are

But you don't

And that's really all that matters, right?

So don't fear me

Don't be afraid to talk to me

But your happiness is all that matters when it comes to you

So not being with me is what will make you happy eventually

You're a very special lady

And I knew the first time I kissed you

That I loved you

Wanted you

To be mine forever"

Seriously?! Don't fear you? Don't be scared of you? Don't you see it? The obsessiveness? The desperation? The possessiveness? I fear you because you hurt me. I fear you will hurt me further. I fear for my safety. There were multiple more messages that rolled in after these ones. One message right after another.

On May 8th, 2018, I decided I needed to get help to make the madness end. I went to the courthouse to ask the Judge to grant me an Emergency Protection Order. My dad feared my safety would be jeopardized further by "poking the bear." I explained to my dad, "Right now, I am safe with you and mom. I am here in your home. I can't stay here forever. I have to go back to

Edmonton to be with my other two children as well. I can't leave them. But if I do not get this order and something much worse happens, what do I have?" At least with this piece of paper, and believe me, I knew very well that it was just a piece of paper, and I knew it would not stop a person from physically harming me if that's what they wanted to do, but it gave the comfort that the police would be at my door in minutes.

The Judge that morning heard everything I had to say. I told him how I was assaulted. I told him I was still scared of my predator's behaviour and his constant harassment, and I was scared for my kids' safety while they were with me should something happen. The Judge agreed. The Judge also asked me if I had gone to the police yet. I told him I was scared to. The Judge told me that what my predator did to me was a very serious assault, and although he could not force me to go to the police, he really recommended that I do. The Judge granted the Emergency Protection Order. I felt a small sense of relief.

My mom helped me find a new place to live with my kids. I was very careful to keep my address from my predator and so were my lawyers and Judges. I had to go back to see a Judge nine days after asking for the protection order. My predator was allowed to defend himself and was able to get the judge to allow FaceTime calls with our son, but still was not to be near my sons or myself. What I didn't know was that my predator would receive a transcript of everything I told the Judge. To me it was fine; it was just something unexpected, as the friend who helped me escape did not want my predator to know he helped me. Without using his name and not really thinking completely straight with nervousness and emotion I said my friend from the shop helped me and it was written in the transcript without using his name. I was upset because I didn't mean to expose him. My predator approached him as soon as he received his copy of the transcript, asking what he thought he was doing. Why did he help me run? My friend told me it was okay.

My predator used his FaceTime calls to try and communicate to me. Instead of talking with his son, he asked if he could talk to me. I was careful when FaceTime'ing with my son to not show a background where he could see anything outside my home; I stayed away from the windows and doors. I was very careful of my surroundings. My predator started harassing me again now that he had a gateway to his son. He started messaging me daily. He asked to talk to his son multiple times a day. To ask me if I could get our son to call my predator's mother. To ask me about things that were "left" at the house after my family and friends went and gathered my things for me when I moved.

On May 22, 2018, I finally decided I needed to tell the police what happened, and what was still happening. I wrote an eleven-page statement of the events. I gave the police a copy of the current protection order, and they asked me if I wanted to press charges. I told them, Yes, I did. I sat there crying while explaining what happened, and while they poked around for more answers, I knew what I needed to do for myself and to make sure that what happened to me didn't happen to someone else.

On June 16, 2018, I had an appointment with the officers who came to my home and helped write a statement. I was to go in and be interviewed and videotaped repeating what I had already written down. I then showed the police that my predator was breaching the protection order with all his messages and that there was no stopping it. The officers told me that he was breaching, and that they would get him today. The arrest happened that afternoon. They didn't keep him, but did charge him with breaching the protection order. I then received a call telling me that the police were not going to charge him with sexual assault because my predator had a different version of events.

I bawled. Of course he would have a different version of events. I asked the officer what more they needed. He said nothing. He just had a different version of events, and there was not enough evidence. My predator told the officers I had mental health issues, was not well, and that I needed help. I was devastated. I started to feel hopeless. What next?

Chapter Seven

NOT GIVING UP

I LAY AWAKE at night, unable to sleep because I felt unsafe. I shuddered knowing he was going to walk free after what he did to me. What he would do to someone else. I started researching on the Internet what my options were. The one thing that popped up and gave me a glimpse of hope was something called a "Private Information." A private Information allows any citizen to lay their own charges on an accused provided they have enough evidence to provide to a Judge or Justice of the Peace. You sit in a Courtroom alone with the Judge/Justice of the Peace, Crown Prosecutor, and the clerk and you take the stand. The evidence you provide is based on probability, and not beyond a reasonable doubt.

I believed wholeheartedly that I had more than enough evidence to prove to a Judge that these events happened. I gathered up all my evidence, starting with messages back in 2017 that showed that he admitted to waking me nightly, touching me, and how it escalated. I gathered up the pictures and voicemails from when I left to show the Judge. I also had to pick the charges I wanted to lay. I chose four. Sexual assault, assault, forcible confinement, and criminal harassment.

Some of the messages I was able to gather out of about four hundred sheets of paper were sexual comments, and messages from him, pressuring me about sex. On October 25, 2017, he wrote, "I feel bad that even though I know how sick you are, I'm cranky from being pent up. Sounds horrible I know but that's part of it I guess. That'll go away I'm sure." December 8, 2017, he wrote an apology for making me uncomfortable because when he laid down in bed beside me he started to masturbate and I left the room. Here are a few more messages from him from December 10, 2017 to April 2018:

> "I feel bad because just being near you sometimes, most of the time, I get turned on by you. I know you can't do anything about that, but I can't control it, either. I don't want you to think it's all I think about."

> "Did you sleep ok at least until I woke you" and "sorry for the aggressive snuggle."

> "I'm sorry about the touching thing as well. Honestly it's like I am in a dream and then I realize what's happening and stop."

> "Did you get off yesterday?"

> "Maybe you should try getting off and see if that helps with the pain."

> "I discovered that I really like the way your panties feel on my skin lol. Not that I'm wearing them or anything."

And a meme, "Women wake up yawning and men wake up with an erection. Coincidence?"

And nine images of him naked, masturbating, coming, and pictures that he captured of threesomes. There was so much evidence.

Before my information session, which was scheduled on August 1, 2018, my predator was granted a parenting order that allowed him to see our son Tuesday and Thursday evenings from 6 p.m.

- 7:30 p.m., and every second weekend from Friday at 6 p.m. to Sunday at 7 p.m. We were to meet in the police station parking lot. He also asked to have FaceTime calls with his son Monday and Wednesday evenings between 7 and 7:10 p.m.

My predator got another gateway to be able to continue harassing me further. The protection order I was granted in June turned into a Mutual Restraining Order. This order meant nothing to my predator. A Mutual Restraining Order was to prevent both parties from directly or indirectly contacting each other. Unfortunately I did not know there could be so many different versions of each order and mine contradicted the parenting order granted. My mutual restraining order also lacked a police clause that would allow them to make an arrest for breaching the order.

My predator took advantage of this. It started with meeting in the parking lot when doing exchanges with our son. My predator found it appropriate to make comments on my looks, for example, "your hair looks really nice today," "you're so pretty," "I love you." These comments were unwanted, but my predator did not stop. Along with these sorts of comments, my predator started bringing me "forgotten" items from when I moved or things he couldn't use. I fully believe this was an excuse just to have contact still, and to get near me.

On July 14, 2018, my predator again did something I was not expecting. I was visiting my parents in Calgary, and around 8 p.m. at night, a friend messaged me to inform me that my predator had made a new public Facebook account. If you don't use Facebook, you have multiple options, two of which are keeping your settings private or making them public. My predator had two accounts now. His first Facebook account was private, and only his friends could see his posts, but this new one was open for anyone to see.

His name popped up on my friend's Facebook feed, sent as a suggestion for a friend. She was curious and opened it. She messaged me after reading what was written, telling me that my name and personal information was written all over this page, along with pictures. I immediately went to see the page that was public. She was right: my name, pictures, and personal information about my health were all over this page. I was so scared. My predator was not stopping.

I called the non-emergency police line after reading the page with my mom. The officer on the phone also was able to see this page and told me he was concerned for my safety. He said he worked with domestic violence and that my predator was showing extreme obsession. This officer also was concerned for my children's well-being. He told me that as soon as I returned home to Edmonton to call the police and tell them about this page. He said to print it off and have it ready for when the police came to my home.

When I returned home on July 15, 2018, I did as the officer said. I called the police upon entering the city limits, and awaited their arrival nervously. When they showed up, I rambled on about this page. Explaining that this was not the first time I have had to call the police. That there were multiple files. They escorted me to the police station where I was to pick up our son from his visitation with his father. When he saw me, he shook his head.

The officers told him to remove the page and asked him to stop posting stuff about me on the page. Immediately, and with the officers there, he removed only the posts on the page. I was crying and thanking the officers. I was terrified of this stupid never-ending behaviour. I took my son, buckled him into his car seat, and took off back home. My predator followed me. He didn't follow me all the way home because when I realized he was following, I didn't go right home. I took a different route after allowing him to pass me. Reassured he was well on his way and not near my part of the city, I felt safe enough to go home.

On July 16, 2018, after his arrest, my predator returned to his public Facebook account to start posting new images and new comments. He didn't stop at just me. My predator started to add pictures of my two older children to his Facebook harassment. Neither my ex-husband nor I make any pictures of our children public, so this made me worry more. My predator knew this, yet he chose to post about them publicly.

On July 22, 2018, I called the police again at around 6:30 p.m. This call was in regards to my predator's continuous posts on this public Facebook account and his breaching the mutual restraining order by emailing me. After calling the police and waiting for them I looked out my window around 9:40 p.m. to notice my predator's vehicle drive by my home! *Holy crap, he found me!* I called the police again. They added it to the call that I previously made at 6:30 p.m. I was so scared bed was completely out of the question. I watched outside my window intently. I watched again as my predator drove by my home around 11:15 p.m. I was stunned. I was terrified he would come banging on my patio door or break a window, as I lived on the ground floor of an apartment building.

The officer who was dispatched to my home didn't come until 9 a.m. the following morning. She empathized with me that my predator was showing some scary behaviour, but she told me that because the Mutual Restraining Order was missing the police clause, there was not much she could do. She told me to keep doing what I was doing by documenting everything, and to call the police as needed. That a file was being made on these calls. I felt discouraged that this was never going to stop. If the

Judge's orders couldn't stop him, and the police couldn't stop him, who could?

Like every other exchange with our son, my predator could not hold his tongue. On July 24, 2018, I went to drop off my son to his father at 6 p.m. in the same police station parking lot where we had been exchanging him for the last month. I had been told by the police to start recording any interactions with my predator so they could catch him breaching the Mutual Restraining Order. I had my recorder on and ready. My predator tried a scare tactic by saying I was acting erratically. I assured my predator I was not erratic. He then asked me if I was trying to have him arrested. I reluctantly told my predator I just wanted him to stop. To stop bugging me, to stop talking to me other than about urgent matters regarding our son, and to stop posting shit all over his public Facebook page.

My predator responded by saying he was not bugging me and that the Facebook page was his to post what he liked. He went on to say that we were together for five years. He wanted us to work together to fix this... he said he was sorry that he hurt me, and that he only wanted to help me get better. He was talking about my illness and the fact that when I got home from the hospital I was supposed to be recovering. (Unfortunately the stress caused upon my return home has hindered my body's healing. My doctors are left uncertain about my state of health.)

I told my predator that it was not about him helping me or pushing me to get well, it was about what he did to me on April 22 and April 23. It was about him waking me nightly for months by groping and grabbing my vagina, by grabbing my butt. My predator admitted to the nightly waking's, to trying to pull my pants down, to locking the bedroom door, (although he said it was for another reason), and to the mistake he made the night of April 23, 2018. My heart was pounding. I thought, *Holy crap,*

I just got him to admit to assaulting me. I called my mom and let her listen to the recording. She told me to call the police. I wanted to wait till later after picking my son up, and after he had gone to bed to call the police and ask them what I should do with this new evidence.

At pick up, my predator had the gall to ask me for a favour, cornering my son and me between vehicles. Can you believe that! He said if I did it he would never ask me for anything else ever... he asked me for a hug. I immediately took a step back and said no. He begged me, please. I again said no, I am not comfortable with that, and backed up. He was so mad. He said, "Fine! Make sure he (our son) sees his sister!" He got into his truck and sped away, squealing his tires as he drove out of the parking lot of the police station. I took this as another threat of suicide.

I picked my son up, put him in his car seat and asked him if he had fun with daddy. I got in my vehicle and drove home. When my son went to bed and I was sure he was asleep, I called the police to inform them of the new evidence. They told me I had to contact the officer to whom I gave my original statement to back in May. I was able to hand in this evidence a few days later.

After calling the police I went on Facebook like I had been doing every single day since my predator started his public page, to see if there was anything new. Of course there was. But the posts this time were not only limited to his public page but also on his private one. These are the messages he posted:

> "I want to say thank you for everything you've given to me, the moments of joy, love, happiness, pleasure and the feeling of trust you showed me.
>
> It's all done now and I understand.
>
> I'm sorry I made you feel hurt.

If this is all my fault, then I am responsible for what happened and I truly deserve what happens.

This is the last time I will say anything.

I truly do love you and knowing how you feel does break my heart. At least now I now know where you stand and what my path is.

Please make sure to kiss our son for me and to give him big hugs before bed.

I hope you can eventually find the happiness I tried to provide you and failed.

All the best to you.

I hope your life eventually becomes what you want.

You're a great mother and the boys are lucky to have you. Treat them well.

Good-bye hun.

I'll miss you bunches."

Going old school with a screwdriver in my hand. (Attached was a you tube clip of the song These arms of Mine-Ottis Redding)

Sounds about right today (Attached was a you tube clip of Bruno Mars song "It Will Rain")

Just have to say, thanks to all the great friends I have for all you do. You're all the best. I appreciate you very much. Cheers!"

My mom also read these posts and advised me to call the police and ask them to do a wellness check, so I called the police on July 25, 2018, and sent the officer, by text message, what was being posted. The officer was also concerned because he felt that these were suicidal thoughts. He called my predator's work and found out he didn't go in. He went to my predator's home and banged on the door. He was there. He told the officer that he was not feeling well, so stayed home. Then he posted this:

> "It's a great thing to have the cops pounding on your door first thing in the morning. I was sleeping for the first time in months and they ruined it.
>
> "Wellness check, eh.
>
> I wonder if anyone ever answers that question they ask honestly, lol.
>
> I'm looking forward to a good weekend with the kids. Fun times before the start of the next chapter of my book."

This was not the first time my predator threatened suicide. Nor would it be the last. The following days my predator posted more crap. More statements about going away, taking things with him, saying it would be a while before he saw his son again. These comments concerned me. It scared me to have to leave my son in his care. My thoughts were only that I didn't want my son harmed by him.

On July 29, 2018, I called the police line again. I told them about these new posts and my concerns for my son. He posted more while my son was with him that evening for his scheduled visit. They dispatched another officer. A female officer called me. I told her what had happened right from the beginning, what had been happening since the Emergency Protection Order was changed to a Mutual Restraining Order, and about the public Facebook page, messages, and emails I was getting. I told her about the constant contact in the police station parking lot. The female officer asked me if my son was with me or with his dad. I told her I had to pick my son up at 7:30 p.m. She told me to call her back as soon as my son was safe with me again. She told me she was going to call my predator and talk to him.

As soon as I had my son, I called the female officer back. When she was done talking to my predator, she told me she gave him a warning. She said she told him he was harassing me and that if he continued to post anything on Facebook, message me, or email me, she would arrest him. She told me that we should now do our exchanges inside the police station. She even offered to do it from her station which was a different one so she could watch my predator. My predator suddenly reverted back to the original parenting agreement, wanting to meet at the same police station where we had been meeting. I agreed, but said it had to be inside the station so that the constant need for him to communicate with me during the exchanges would end. The last thing my predator said to me when I picked up my son was, "Can I be completely honest with you. I am never going to be okay with you being with someone else. That is my problem." Sadly, meeting inside the police station did not stop my predator from approaching me, and still trying to communicate with me.

Chapter Eight

THE ARREST

MY PREDATOR CONTINUED his nonsense. His constant disregard for any authority was terrifying me. Nothing was stopping this creep. The officer told me to update her every time he posted something, emailed me, or messaged me. I don't think she realized what she was asking, but I did what she wanted.

After speaking to the female officer, my predator started with an apology email. The officer said to give him a chance. I said okay. At 6:55 p.m., his fingertips must not have been able to tell his brain "stop it," because he was back on his public Facebook page posting more comments.

> "Frustrated. Lost and angry. Still love you so much and my hands are tied. I still don't understand why the hate is there. I understand the hurt, the disappointment, and even the anger. Hate is such a strong thing to try to feel. I'll never be able to feel that. Not towards you. I guess that's my problem though. You know what you think you know. You see what you see. And that's not me."

Before 11 p.m., there was more:

> "I miss you so much. Hope you have a good sleep; you're in my thoughts every day. And I love you dear, good night."

I wish I could hold you just one more time and that would make my
life complete really.

A meme "I just want you to miss me like I do you and hold
me like you used to. I'm scared I'm waiting for something that
won't happen."

Yes, Predator, hold your friggin' breath. You will never get to
hold me again. You will never get to touch me ever again. You
lost my trust, my respect, and your dignity by just not keeping
your hands to yourself. You did not respect my boundaries, by
hurting me.

August 1, 2018 was finally the day I had to provide my private
information before a Judge. I was not nervous. I had everything
ready. I had to sit outside the courtroom and wait for my turn.
There were many cases before mine. I think the waiting was the
worst. While waiting my friend from down east messaged me.
I could not believe my eyes! My predator publicly posted four
very intimate half naked images of me for all to see. I had no
words. I started to cry. Two officers were sitting beside me. I
showed them what my predator posted. They immediately told
me to call the police when I was done at the court house. What
the hell was he thinking! This is where I learned my hard lesson.
You think you know someone. You trust them with everything.
Be careful!

My name finally got called to go into the courtroom. They
closed the door behind me and put a sign on the door saying
closed for private matter. I bravely faced the Judge who then
asked me to take the stand. I brought my massive folder up with
me. I had everything in numerical order of dates and times. The
Judge first asked me some questions about who I was, who my
predator was to me, and touched on why I was there.

As the Judge went through page by page the papers I brought as my evidence, she occasionally relayed what she was reading to the crown prosecutor. It took two hours for the Judge to patiently go through all the papers. I even showed the Judge the newest posts with my half naked pictures. She told me to show the crown prosecutor when we were done because that was a criminal offence. When she was done, she asked me to sit down at the defenders table. I did. She spoke directly to the crown prosecutor and told them she believed that this did, in fact, happen. The Judge laid three of the four charges I asked to be laid. One Sexual Assault, one Assault and one for forcible confinement. I had also asked for a Criminal Harassment charge, but the Judge could see by all the posts, and because I told her the police were building up a file against my predator for his constant harassment that he would soon be charged for that.

I walked out of the courtroom with the crown prosecutor, showing her the images my predator posted. She also advised me to call the police. As soon as I left the building I emailed the officer who warned my predator not to be posting anything further. I also added the other most recent posts in the emails.

This one was his very next post after posting the intimate images:

> "Hi. How's your day going today? I hope you're doing well. I miss talking to you and hearing your voice. I miss your smiling face."

And then,

> "I really hope someday you will be my friend again. I miss that the most of all. Among other things, but that is what I miss most."

With everything that had happened up to this point I had never grieved the loss of the relationship I had with my predator. I didn't regret leaving, I didn't regret calling the police or reporting my abuse, and I didn't regret trying to keep my kids safe and protected. Is it weird I did not grieve? After almost five years and having a child together should I have felt anything when leaving him other than fear and guilt for my kids? I don't know. What's right and what's wrong? Is there supposed to be a specific way you deal with loss of an abuser?

On August 2, 2018, I had to face my abuser for what I thought would be the last time for a while. It was also my birthday. My predator couldn't help himself. It's like he has no off-switch. When dropping off my son for an exchange, he and I were sitting in the common area waiting for his dad. When my predator arrived, he was sure to wish me a happy birthday. I didn't say a word. I stayed in my seat and I waited for my predator and my son to leave the station.

My heart sank every single time my child had to go alone with my predator. My predator took to his Facebook account again that night. He tried to make me feel guilty.

"On April 29th, I was going to ask permission. This Saturday August 4th, in front of our friends and family, at a party to celebrate your birthday, I was going to ask the question.

Will you marry me?

After five years together, the story's next chapter was to start.

Then came the confusion and miscommunication that was April 23rd.

How I wish that night never happened. How I wish I didn't find that silly toy. Clearly used the previous night or that morning.

One more try, I thought; if she's doing it alone she may be open to it today. We had a great night shopping for stuff for the kids. Winter planning. Hats and mitts for all of them. It was a mistake, I guess. That day I regret alone. I wish you would have just said, not tonight, so we could move forward.

But alas you did not. And I did not read your cues. I'm sorry.

I wanted this to happen since I first kissed you. Since I first knew I loved you."

My predator still does not see that what he did was a problem. Someone who held onto their pants so that they could not be removed for a fifteen-minute span should have been a very good cue to stop. I didn't say stop because just the day before, the word didn't mean a damn thing. I didn't feel that even if I had said no that my predator was going to stop. I was terrified and felt frozen inside while I fought my predator to keep my pants on.

Miscommunication? Really? No, I don't think so. I think my predator wanted sex so bad that had I not caved and given him head I would have been raped. Maybe not that night, but in the nights to follow.

After picking my son up, getting him home and into bed, I went to sit outside, in the dark, to await my predator's drive by. While I was waiting, the officer messaged me to ask me to write a statement of events for her. As she messaged me, sure enough, my predator drove by my home. The second time, I tried to take a picture, but missed, but the security cameras I installed on July 23, 2018 captured his vehicle. I think I scared him off with the flash of my camera. The female officer said that she would be arresting him on August 5th for criminally harassing me.

A few more days I thought. Just a few more days.

I couldn't wait for the harassment to end. Knowing the end was coming was hard to keep to myself. The messages on Facebook never stopped.

"I was sitting here and going over some pictures today. I can't believe some of the things we did. Our walk through the river valley was one of my favourite days.

That November day in our room, black sheets hanging. I love those ones.

The walk through white mud park with the kids.

All great times.

Remember our walk after the bar? Hear the coyotes howl?

So many memories. All gone."

Of course I remember these things. My predator for months has done nothing but remind me daily, and shown the world these images. My predator was now aware something was up as the officer had talked to him and asked him to come into the station. He couldn't help himself; texting me a one last ditch effort text message at 12:10 a.m. on August 5, 2018.

"My dearest,

I was going to call you, but I knew you would not answer. I would give anything to hear your voice one more time. Anything to hear you say you love me. You forgive me and you want to try again.

I know this is not going to happen. As much as this breaks my heart, I told you I would never hate you. I would love you forever and I meant it.

You're moving on with your life. I know some part of you still loves me. It's not enough for you. I understand.

I will never be able to see you with someone else. It will tear me apart. I know it will happen someday. I can't be around to see it. So I won't be. You want me out of your life, you've tried to have me arrested on numerous occasions. Whatever the depth of your pain is, please look after it. You need to be there for our son now.

I can't go on like this. I love him so much as well as all the kids. They will be better off without me now. When you left and said the things you did, it broke me. Made me different. I don't like it. I will always love you and I hope someday you can find it in your heart to think kindly of me.

Please make sure that our son gets to spend time with my other children. They love him so much and things will be hard enough on them now. Don't hate me. Please.

We should be celebrating our engagement, but instead I will give you the freedom from me you seek. Hold my boy tight, and tell him every day how much I love him.

I'm going to send him a little video so he doesn't forget me. Please let him watch it. Be good to the boys and please don't let them continue to think of me the way they do now. I love them and I hope you will let them know that.

Baby I'm so sorry if anything I did really hurt your heart. You know that I would never intentionally hurt you. I love you.

From the first kiss in the hot tub to the last loving stroke of your hand across my cheek that Wednesday night. My love for you never stopped growing. I'm sorry. So sorry. Given your feelings now, I don't know if this will hurt you or not. I hope not, as this is not my intent.

I am not home and won't be so no need to call anybody to help me. It's beyond that now. What you feel, or felt, or didn't doesn't matter now. Move on, baby. Get happy. And grow. Seek the help you need to take your next step in life.

My time with you is done, I hope you find what you seek someday. It is obvious I was not the puzzle piece you needed to fit with, and I was not the one to fulfill your needs, as hard as I tried.

I love you always

I miss you forever

As long as I'm living

My baby you'll be."

Another attempt to try to reel me in. To make me feel guilty to get me to stop the charges coming his way. Using a saying that I only said to my children as I tucked them into bed each night. So delusional. Please don't misunderstand my lack of sympathy for my predator's threats of suicide, as I believe suicide is something very serious, but my predator had threatened this multiple times, with never any action.

I was at a friend's baby shower. My kids were having fun playing at a camp ground amid the smells of freshly cooked hot dogs and hamburgers on the barbecue. There must have been at least fifty people there. I received a call from the officer who was going to make the arrest. I knew she just worked the night before, but she was up because she received a call from another officer, her friend, who called to tell her my predator called in to the police line to tell them that he "accidentally" sent me a text message.

First off do you see the amount written in that message? He didn't just send this message. He did in fact send a short video for our son. But then he also sent a message the following morning asking me to ignore the messages, his desperate attempt prompted him to also ask me publicly to ignore the message because he already had to see "my female officer" that night.

The female officer told me she just wanted me to know what he did, and reassured me that she was going to make the arrest that night. I could not wait for this to end. All day I waited.

We enjoyed our time with our friends and had about an hour's drive home. When I got home I got the kids to bed as I knew that the officer would be messaging me to ask me questions during his arrest.

Before I heard from her, my friend from down east who was also anticipating his arrest, sent me a message showing me that my predator had deleted the public Facebook profile prior to him going to see the female officer. I was sure to let her know that this page was in fact gone. Thank God I had captured everything, with the help of friends and family. The police, lawyers, and Judge all asked me to capture it all with the help of these other people.

Finally the message I was waiting for. "He's here." I started to cry. The female officer told me that she made the arrest after interviewing him. She told me that she was charging him with Criminal Harassment, Posting Intimate Images online without permission, obstruction of justice and breach of the Mutual Restraining Order.

I told her Thank you. For the first night in months, I felt like I would be able to sleep and feel some sort of safety. She requested no bail, but unfortunately the following day my predator was released on bail conditions. My heart sank. From July 29, 2018 when I first talked with this officer till his arrest on August 5, 2018 there were 37 new posts on Facebook, six text messages, seven emails, and a video that he sent after being asked to stop harassing me by the officer, and told that if it continued he would be arrested. Many people thought that perhaps he needed a psych assessment.

The bail conditions were slightly confusing. It stated that my predator was not to have any indirect or direct contact with me or my son. But there was a clause in it that said he would not be breaching the order should there be a parenting order in place that was granted by the Court of Queen's Bench or other competent jurisdiction.

I was told I was not to continue the visitations by one officer, and so I didn't. I went to see my family in Calgary with my son. While we were there, I received another call from another officer telling me that I was breaching the parenting order, and asked me why. I explained that I was told that I was not to bring my son to his visitations as per the bail conditions, where it stated no direct or indirect contact with my son. The officer told me I would not be arrested, but that following Tuesday the visitations needed to continue as set out in the parenting order. I was so scared. I told him I was sorry, but I was doing what I was told.

The officer also told me he understood my position and wanted to help until I could get back into court to have the parenting order changed. He told me that from this point forward, so that I did not have to face my predator, I would arrive at the station first, ahead of the drop off time, and I would have time to go into the station with my son and wait in the interview room. The officer then said that when my predator came into the building he would wait in the common area while the officer who was on duty came to the interview room to get my son and take him to his dad. This would reverse at pick up times with my predator in the interview room.

This worked okay for a bit. Until my predator got brave again and started to follow me in his vehicle again.

Sunday Sept 9, 2018

My predator was waiting in the interview room with our son. While I waited for an officer to go and get my son and bring him to me I could hear my predator tell the officer he was in a hurry. The officer then brought me my son. I was always quick to get out of the station and get my son in his car seat so we could leave. But on this particular day, my predator came out of the station as I was finishing putting our son into his car seat in my vehicle. I got into my vehicle and left the lot, heading north towards Windermere Blvd.

My predator was behind me. We do have to travel the same way to get to Anthony Henday. My predator lives south and I live in the Westend.

We both turned right onto Windermere Blvd which then I was in the far-left lane and my predator in the lane beside me we then both turned left onto Terwilliger Drive North. My predator stayed in the right lane until the very last second before he should have gone East on Henday. I was still in the left lane to go West on Henday. He pulled in behind me. He followed me onto Henday west until Cameron Heights; then he sped past me and continued on his way.

Friday Sept 21, 2018

I took my son to the police station for a scheduled drop off at 6 p.m. It was an unusual exchange as the constable was already outside the station. He said, why don't we just do the exchange out here? My son was hesitating going with the Constable to go to see his dad. After a few minutes, I said to the constable, I will walk with my son, but I need you to walk beside me. He said he would.

As we were walking toward my predator, he told my son to hurry as he had to get his other two kids who lived in the other end of the city. I was able to leave the police station before my predator, but he was quick to catch up with me on Windermere

Blvd, heading east towards Terwilliger Drive. This time he stayed behind me. He followed me from Windermere Blvd, onto Terwilliger drive north, turned West on Henday behind me and followed me all the way to Whitemud Drive before he then turned to head East on Whitemud. His kids would have been at their mother's house again on the opposite end of the city. I am unsure why my predator would have followed me all the way to the Whitemud to only head back all the way to the other side of the city.

I drove back to the police station to talk to the Constable. I explained that this was not the first time he had followed me. The Constable said, the problem is that we cannot say where he is allowed to drive and my predator could just lie and say he had to stop at West Edmonton Mall first before going to get his other children. I told him I understood, but that it was still frustrating when I know he is indeed following me. I felt completely intimidated by my predator as he followed me.

Friday October 5, 2018

I went to the police station for another scheduled exchange at 6 p.m. where I was dropping off my son to my predator for his weekend visitation. I was in the interview room. I stayed in the police station and waited until my predator left. I watched him leave the police station parking lot to go into the next parking lot. I waited a few extra minutes waiting to see if he would come back out of the lot. He didn't. When I felt it was safe I went to my vehicle and got in. As I was about to leave the police station parking lot, my predators vehicle appeared and pulled out of the parking lot beside me. He was driving ahead of me. We both headed towards Windermere Blvd. We both turned right onto Windermere Blvd. My predator stayed in the far-left lane to turn onto Terwilliger Drive North. I stayed in the right lane, thinking that, if he was going to turn left and go west on Henday again, I would just go straight on Terwilliger Drive and take Whitemud West home. When we got onto Terwilliger Drive North my predator started in the left lane. I stayed right. Just before the turn to go east on Anthony Henday, my predator, still driving ahead of me, moved to the right lane. I then thought, okay, he is going to go East on Henday; I can now just take my regular route and go West on Henday, so I moved into the left lane. As soon as I moved into the left lane my predator followed suit, still driving ahead of me, and moved back into the left lane. He ended up going into the turning lane to turn left to go West on Henday. So I again moved back into the right lane, and decided to go straight up Terwilliger Drive north to take Whitemud home. I was watching to see if my predator would pull back in behind me. I didn't see him pull out so I thought okay he is done playing games. I was wrong. Just before I was arriving at the last set of lights by the BP on Terwilliger Drive, before itturns to go onto Whitemud, I thought I could see my predator's vehicle behind a white van that was behind me. At that set of light the van turned left and sure enough it was my predator's vehicle behind me. He then got into the right lane before the turn to go East on Whitemud. I was able to stop my vehicle safely on the road, and capture the predator's vehicle pass mine, got a picture of his plate and a picture of him exiting to go Whitemud east. This was around 6:11 p.m.

My predator continued to follow me with my children in the vehicle. My kids became aware of what he was doing, and they were asking me why I was taking odd ways home. My oldest, who was ten at the time, saw my predator's vehicle drive by us when I turned onto a completely different road—he asked if he had been following us this whole time, and if that was the reason why we had been taking different ways. I told him yes.

There is nothing that you can hide from kids when they are so observant.

These incidents were documented and an officer I had been working with since June tried to catch my predator following us. Unfortunately I think my predator assumed something was up and although was in the left lane as usual to follow me, buggered off and went straight. The officers followed me home and talked with me a bit. They said, "We tried." They told me they would drive around a bit to see if there was any chance he was around. That made me feel a little safer knowing they had our best interests at heart.

On October 9th, 2018, my predator and I had a court date set for the second time to amend the Mutual Restraining Order and have it changed to just a Restraining Order for him. To my amazement, my predator chose not to show up. I got my four-page, very detailed Restraining Order, it now had a police clause and many other restrictions, so that my predator would be easily breached by police should they need to arrest him. I was so happy. Finally I had an order that coincided with the bail conditions. The last thing that still needed to change was the parenting order.

Chapter Nine

WHEN A SON
FEARS HIS FATHER

MY SON STARTED his visitations with his dad in June of 2018, after the parenting order was worked out and was granted. Up until this point, the Emergency Protection Order only allowed my son to FaceTime with his dad. My son was excited to see his dad. I was glad that he got to see his dad. I didn't want to see him because of what he did to me, and so I was nervous for my son's safety with his father. The question, *He did this to me—is it possible he could do this to his child,* stayed in the back of my mind. *Would he use our son to get to me?* I only wanted my son safe and loved.

In June, after the visits started, my son started saying strange things when he came home. Keep in mind that he was still only three at the time. The first strange thing he said was, "Mommy you don't need to check my bum." I asked him why I would need to check his bum. He said, "No, I said you don't need to check my bum." I thought, *Okay did he have a poop at daddy's and was there still something there bugging him?* The next time he used the bathroom, I checked to see if there was anything there. I saw nothing. I wrote it down in my notes in my phone, with the date and time my son made this strange comment.

My son was never excited to sit on the phone and FaceTime with his father. At the age of three, his attention span was short, and he would rather be doing other things, like watch a show or play with his brothers. His father would keep him on the phone no less than twenty minutes. He would ask our son what he did that day, where he went that day. If my son avoided the questions, he would ask over and over and over again. My son was busy and would run from room to room. I held the phone so that we could be careful of the windows and views my predator would be able to see. One time he said, "I don't see what the big deal is if I just see out your window." *Pardon me! It's a big frigging deal! I am hiding from you!*

A couple of weeks went by, and during the exchanges, my predator would try to communicate with me. It was never about our son. On July 5, 2018, after another visit with his dad, my son had something unusual to say. My three-year-old son was holding a pencil, and he told me he was going to shove the pencil up my bum. He was actually trying to shove the pencil up my bum through my pants. I took the pencil and asked him where he learned that. He said I don't know. I told him we don't do things like that, and it's not okay. I told him we don't touch other people's bums.

I had tried, from the time I filed my report with the police, and when getting the Emergency Protection Order, to have someone talk to my children. I wanted to know if anything had ever happened to them, and I provided my reasons for concern. My older two children were only two and five when my predator came into their lives. I talked to Child Family Services, and at the time, they saw no need for concern, no need to talk to my kids yet. I called around to see where I could take my kids to see a counsellor. The wait times were very long.

On July 13, 2018, when dropping my son off at 6 p.m. to see his father, he tried to strike up a conversation as usual—asking me if I was ever going to forgive him, and telling me that I was angry and I needed to let that anger out. My predator didn't know that I had been on a waiting list for months to see a therapist because of what he did to me. My predator didn't know I couldn't eat or sleep. My predator told me to take my anger out on him in the parking lot of the police station—he was holding our three-year-old son at the time—asking me to hit him, kick him, and scream at him, but to just let it all out. That it would make me feel better. I calmly walked away but was pissed that he chose to ask this of me while holding our three-year-old son in his arms! I am not a hitter. I use words instead, and this time, I chose to bite my tongue and leave.

On July 22, 2018, my three-year-old woke from his first nightmare. He told me he had a bad dream—he was sobbing. Telling me that daddy was a monster. I know that kids have nightmares. I know that kids see things sometimes even if we try to protect them from it, but my three-year-old, who had been potty trained for several months, was now starting to have accidents after seeing his dad, and now nightmares. My concerns grew. I booked an appointment with my son's pediatrician. I told him my concerns and I asked him to document them all. His doctor wanted to run tests on him to rule out anything medical going on. Those tests all came back completely fine. There were no medical reasons for my son's new accidents.

In October, my three-year-old son started asking me to kiss body parts. He asked me to kiss his boobies and the boobies of his Captain America action figure. I told him that nobody should kiss his boobies. I again asked him where he learned this. His response was, "I don't know." After every pick up, he said that he thought he would never see me again. I had to reassure him after every single visit that his mommy would always be there to pick him up. Every single time. More of his comments concerned me, and I reported each one to his doctor. He started complaining of a sore penis and bum, and he started to take his pants and underwear down in front of complete strangers. When I asked if he had to go to the bathroom, or if it hurt to pee, he said no.

On October 31, 2018, I took my kids trick or treating. We went to my friend's house on our way home. She had to work with my predator, who at one time was constantly stalking her at work, too. She told me that my predator told her that, on his last visit, my son told him that he was scared of him. This just opened a whole new set of worries to my son's unusual behaviour. My son started to cry at visits, not leaving the room anymore when the police came to get him to bring him to his father. When picking my son up at daycare I always told him that he would get to go see daddy today. I tried to make it sound exciting. It was becoming tougher to listen to my child scream that he didn't want to see his daddy, and not to leave him alone with daddy. This went on for a couple of weeks and worsened over time.

My son, at one of his last visits, would not leave the interview room. Trying to coax a three-year-old to go somewhere they are adamant they don't want to be is very difficult. I had to face my predator, while inching my son closer to him in the police station lobby. My son kept saying, "No, I am not going with daddy." I got closer and closer. I promised my son he would be okay and that mommy would be back for him. I told him he would have fun at daddies. My son was still adamant that he was not going, and he pulled away from his father when my predator tried to grab him by the collar of his coat. My son hid behind me, saying No. On the second grab, he got him. He picked up my son and told him he was acting ridiculous. He started to carry my son out of the police station, and all the while my son was wailing, "I want my mommy! I want my mommy!" I walked back into the room where my other two children were waiting for me quietly. My middle son got up; he seemed to know that was a hard moment, and gave me a huge hug.

I called my son's pediatrician to inform him that my son now was terrified to be with his father. The doctor told me it was time to get Child Family Services involved, something I had been trying to do for months. He told me to call them, too. I didn't know there were others who had already called. On November 14, 2018, later in the evening, I received a call from Child Family Services after they did a little investigating into another open file on my predator. The lady I spoke to told me I needed to immediately—the following day—get another Emergency Protection Order for my son, and to include myself and my other children on the order. This scared me further.

The next morning I got on the phone to start making calls. I went that afternoon to ask another Judge to grant me a protection order to protect my son from his father. I told the Judge everything I had told his pediatrician, and that Child Family Services now had an open assessment, and were doing an investigation on my children and the two other children of my predator. I was shaking so bad from fear.

I was not afraid of the Judge or telling the Judge what had been happening—the constant stalking, the constant intimidation, my son's experiences and the concerns I had. I was petrified that once my predator knew Child Family Services was involved, we would be at bigger risk than we had been this whole time. I had been prepared over the last several months that I could possibly end up in a body bag, based on my predator's ongoing attacks and harassment, but I would be damned if I would let him get his monster hands on my children.

I was right to be scared. The Judge granted me the order immediately. My lawyer was with me, and also a worker from victim services. The Judge told me he very much believed that my son and I would be in immediate danger once my predator was served these papers he would not get to see his son. Again the tears flowed. This was all overwhelming.

After my lawyer and victim services left the courtroom, they asked me if I had a safe place to go with my son. I told them I could figure something out. I called a friend and we planned to stay there, but first I went home alone to grab the items I felt we needed, not knowing how long I would not be allowed back in my home. I also had to call my ex-husband and father of my two older children to see if he could take the kids a day earlier so that they were safe. I gave him a copy of the order as well as the kids' school and daycare. I had two extra copies made to carry with me.

We were safe for one night. The next day my son and I headed to Calgary. I knew we would be safe with my family. I went to the RCMP office to give them a copy of the order. They told me they were aware of what was going on. They told me to call 9-1-1 immediately should my predator come to Calgary. It was a very quiet nine days. It was almost more worrisome that my predator was so quiet, as opposed to him following and stalking me. At least when he was following and stalking me I knew where he was.

Nine days later I had to face my predator again in a courtroom to ask the Judge to keep the EPO in place. The Judge was firm with my predator when he told her he had not seen his son. She did not sympathize with him, but asked him if he had a lawyer and if he knew how serious the allegations against him were. He angrily said "I do." The Judge allowed the EPO to stay in place and said it would go to a hearing. That hearing was not until January 11, 2019. My predator, while walking away from the Judge said, "This is fucking ridiculous," under his breath while walking past me.

For two months, my son and I bounced around between friends in Edmonton and my family in Calgary, unsure of our next move. Victim services told me they really wanted me to relocate, as they felt we were not safe at our current home, the home we hadn't set foot in for two months. Not being able to afford to move again, I was torn. I had to go again and apply through Alberta Works for the Fleeing Abuse Benefits. Thankfully they granted this to me for the second time.

I was able to find a home very quickly after Christmas. We moved to a place that was off the ground floor, unlike our current home. I had two victim services people working with me at that time, one to help with family court matters, and one to help me through the criminal matters. Each of them checked in regularly to see how I was holding up, and to see if we were still safe.

My son does not ask for his dad. He does not ask me to kiss body parts, he has not attempted to shove any item in anyone's body, and he has not wet the bed. He has only mentioned that when he was at his daddy's house, he was scared of him and hid. No kid should have to be so scared of their parent that they have to hide. No parent should scare their child so much that they scream not to go with that other parent. My son is happy right now. He doesn't feel my fear, nor my stress or worry every time I had to face my predator. He doesn't cry because he worries about not seeing me again. He is so happy.

The days leading up to January 11, 2019 were hard. I struggled with my mental health and dealing with all the stuff that was to come. My son's safety was all I wanted. A few days before court, I met with my new lawyer, who would be helping me with the emergency protection order process. She told me that unless I could get Child Family Services to come and vouch for me in court, there was a huge possibility that the protection order would be dropped by the Judge. I called the Child Family Services worker who assessed my children. She told me that none of the kids disclosed anything and that she didn't think she needed to be at court with me unless it was to support me. I told her if she could come and tell the Judge about the new allegations that had just come out that it would be very helpful. The worker told me that I knew just as much as she did and that there was not much more she could do for me. She told me she thought my son was at possible risk of being hurt when alone with his father, but that nothing had happened yet.

Can you imagine being told that a professional believes that there is a risk to your child, but that they could not help?! I was beyond livid. I was scared and frustrated. I didn't give up hope. My next contact was the officer that had been working with me since the end of June. I emailed him, basically begging for his assistance. I told him I needed someone to vouch for me, and that what I told the Judge is true. The officer told me he would try to come.

On January 11, 2019, I arrived at court unsure and vibrating with fear. My predator gave me a big smirk. The kind of smirk that says, "I got this." My predator is cocky. I am very sure he thinks he walks on water and is untouchable. I went into the courtroom with two victim services workers and my lawyer. My lawyer sat in the front while the two victim services workers and I took a seat in the farthest row in the back, away from my predator. While sitting there, waiting for the Judge to come into the courtroom, I was nervous, not knowing if the officer would be able to attend or not. To my amazement, the officer called. I answered my phone and left the courtroom. The officer asked what floor I was on. I felt a small sense of relief. *He came,* I thought!

I waited for the officer to arrive on my floor with one of the victim services workers. My lawyer came out, too. This officer was under no obligation to go this far beyond the call of duty, to show up in a courtroom and speak on behalf of someone without being subpoenaed. The officer came because he knew what was in another complainant's file that was under investigation. That complainant wanted to help keep us safe. . The four of us walked back into the courtroom, with me beside the officer, and the look on my predator's face was now one of uncertainty. The officer sat right beside my predator while I went back to my seat with the victim services workers.

The Judge came into the room and I could not stop vibrating. My anxiety was so high. This could go either way. We were there for an oral hearing (basically, the two parties have equal opportunity to tell the Judge their side of things), and then the Judge decides whether or not the protection order stays in place or is no longer needed). We were one of the first to go up. Our names were called and I tried to stand up, but my legs were shaking badly. *Stay strong,* I told myself.

The Judge graciously heard what the officer had to say. He gave my predator options, one of which was for the Judge to take the time to read my predators affidavit that day while court took a short break and then he would make a decision regarding the EPO or, and he highly recommended this while directly looking at my predator, to wait until the next court date, (coming up the following week, on January 17, 2019), for the parenting order to be changed. The Judge said that the Family Law Judge could then also decide if the order was needed, but made another oral hearing date for the protection order, just in case. That oral hearing date was set for March 1, 2019. I was so grateful to the officer for coming. I was so grateful for the Judge, who seemed leery of my predator now. The next step was to convince the Family Law Judge why my son needed to have new visitation rules while with his father. I was asking for supervised visitation and sole decision-making for my now four-year-old son. I thought with all that was going on this was a fair request.

On January 16, 2019, I got an email from my lawyer, telling me that my predator was going to ask for yet another adjournment at court the following day. I was kind of glad, but confused about why he was going to fight the protection order, but not fight for the parenting rights immediately. The Judge welcomed the adjournment request. The Judge also told my predator that he had to give me time to respond to his affidavit, which he was expected to provide. Court was re-scheduled for February 12, 2019. That gave him almost three weeks to respond to my initial request from December 6, 2018. My predator filed his affidavit on February 8, 2019—he left me with only one day to respond.

The things he asked for were things I was not willing to budge on, like him having my son for overnight visits, and doing exchanges at the daycare instead of at a police station. What would happen if our son had a fever and could not go to daycare or during holidays when the daycare is closed? It also brought him closer to our new home and would give him an easier opportunity to find our home and stalk it again. "No! Not happening," I told my lawyer. He also wanted me to pay the costs of his missed time from work. He had adjourned every single order, not me. I again told my lawyer, "No. I won't pay him anything. Not for court, when he has made every effort to extend the dates, and now again. No. "

So many things to wait for. So many times of uncertainty. Praying, please keep my baby safe. I again turned to the officer, asking him to come to court again on February 12, 2019. He told me he would ask his boss and let me know. The hardest part is waiting. My lawyer was starting to sound hopeless. I told her, "I have not come all this way to fight for my kids' safety only to give up hope."

Chapter Ten

THE ALLEGATIONS

DO YOU REMEMBER I told you that my predator no longer spoke to his sister? I have debated back and forth whether or not I should write about this. But how will you know the whole story, if I hold it back?

A couple of years ago before I left my predator, on November 7, 2016 at 10:49 p.m. I received a private Facebook message from someone who was not on my friends list. I didn't know who this person was, but I accepted the message the following morning because these words caught my eye.

"Hello. I am writing you this message with concerns for the well-being of your children."

That one sentence got my attention and I had to open it to see what the rest of the message contained.

"I want you to know that your partner is a pedophile. He has molested many people including myself. I know that you have no idea who I am, but I want you to know that your partner is my so-called Uncle. He left Nova Scotia to try to hide from his past. It has been many years since my family confronted him, leading him to leave the province. Since that time, there have been a few more people come forward with the terrible things this person has done to us. As a survivor, I feel you should know that your children are at risk. He has abused both males and females. His ex-wife is also aware that this happened, but chose not to listen. Do with this information as you wish, but I want you to know this is all coming to light, and he can no longer hide."

Holy crap, I thought. Who is this and why are they saying such horrible things? I was stumped. I continued to fold laundry and ponder what I had just read. My heart was racing. I messaged our mutual friend—the one my predator introduced me to earlier in our relationship—asking what she would do with the information I had just received. She told me to ask this person for a police file number and to prove it. I had not seen any behaviour that would strike me in an odd way or cause me to be concerned for my children's safety with him. My children loved him, and didn't seem to fear him.

I had to confront him. I had to know who this person was—this person who was writing these awful things. My predator's mother was visiting us from Nova Scotia, and this was my first time meeting her and getting to know her. I privately confronted my predator in our bedroom, showing him the message I had just read. I asked him who the hell it was. He confirmed that it was his niece, daughter of the sister he and his family no longer spoke to. My predator then became angry. He hurried out to the kitchen to tell his mother about the message. I followed and watched her reaction. She was angry, too. She said, "Why can't she stop lying." She was cursing up and down, my predator was following suit. My predator said his niece had mental issues, and was crazy. I asked him if this is why he no longer spoke to his sister. He said, "Yes, because it's not true. She has been doing this for a very long time, and she needs to stop." Then he asked me if I believed him. I was stupid to believe him.

The truth was that I didn't know what to believe. I didn't know this niece. I had never even heard of her before. Before I was sexually assaulted by my predator, I had never had reason to believe my children were at risk of being harmed by him. It definitely made me talk to my children, and ask them in a round-about way if anyone had ever touched them inappropriately. I am not proud of my reaction to the message from my predator's niece. I dismissed what she said, and brushed it off because I did not see my predator that way at the time. I didn't see him as a monster. I didn't think he could hurt a child.

After being sexually assaulted by my predator, and after leaving him, I knew I had to try to message his niece again to see what she was trying to tell me before. I had to see if my kids were, in fact, at risk. My predator had reported her message on my Facebook, and it took me a month to find out who she was. I only knew her mother's first name. My brother helped, my friend tried to help, and so had my sister. On June 3, 2018, I found her. I immediately messaged her, scared of what she might say, because I had not believed her before. I had to see it again. I had to ask questions. I was worried she might not respond to my message, leaving me to wonder even more if my kids were at risk. I now wondered what my predator's family had to hide—why were they protecting him? My question now was, what did they do?

To my surprise, my predator's niece did answer. I told her that I needed to know what she was trying to tell me before, and that I did believe her; I believed she had been victim of sexual abuse by him. She again wrote that my predator molested her. That there were many others (all family) that had experienced the same thing. I started crying, reading what she was writing. My mom was sitting with me. We were both shocked. I don't think my sexual abuse had finished setting in yet. Now I had to worry whether my children had experienced the same form of abuse from someone I had let into their lives. I was terrified to know the answer.

I tried to talk to my children but also was cautious not to ask directly using my predator's name in case any of this ever went to court. I never wanted my kids to say, "Mommy said her "predator" touched us." I looked high and low for a professional who could ask my children these questions and I got nowhere. I called Child Protection but was told that unless my kids have disclosed something, I was already doing everything I could to keep them safe. The anxiety I felt every time I had to leave my son with his father was intense. It was almost unbearable at times, making me want to take my son and run.

The niece and I decided it would be best that neither of us discuss the details of what happened to each of us. I did tell her that he had sexually assaulted me, and that I had filed a complaint with the police. She really wanted to go to the police, too, so that she could help me keep my children safe. I think she struggled. I had just reopened her past. I am sure all her memories came flooding back, and she didn't know how to process it all. I believed her when she said she would go to the police. It took some time before she went to file her second report with the police.

On June 30, 2018, when I had an officer come to my home because my predator was breaching the Mutual Restraining Order I told the officer everything, including the messages from my predator's niece. He believed me. He wanted to know how to contact her, and he did contact her. He also asked her to go to the police. I knew this would not be easy for her. Her mother's entire family had disowned them because she believed her daughter was molested by her very own brother. I can't wrap my head around that. How does a grandmother not believe her own grandchild? Or an Aunt? Or an Uncle? I did not believe her at first, but I didn't have a clue who this person was. This poor girl, her entire life, had not been believed. I felt more guilt for that than I had for what happened to me, or for any guilt I should have felt when I left him. I felt the most guilt for my children, and for not believing her.

In September 2018, I received a call from the officer I had spoken with in regards to the messages with my predator's niece. He informed me that she did in fact go to the police, and filed a report. That there was now an investigation going on in regards to these allegations. Fear struck me again. My then three-year-old had to be alone with my predator. The officer tried to get Child Family Services involved, but they told him the same thing they had told me when I called them back in June. It's the mother's obligation to keep her children safe. The mother needs to take them to a pediatrician, the mother needs to file to have the parenting order revised, the mother needs to make sure the kids go to therapy.

All I could think was I was trying to get my kids to therapy. I didn't have one lead for a therapist who was willing to talk to my kids. It was not easy to get the parenting order changed. My lawyer, however, was working on it. I had taken my kids to the doctors, and I had the doctor document all the strange comments from my youngest son. I was so scared. I couldn't fathom what he would do to my child—what he had done to my other two children—but I had to keep it quiet for a bit. I felt immense fear that as soon as my predator knew about these allegations and the investigation, he would come for my son and me.

My son began to fear his dad. Began to have accidents, began to cry for hours before going to see his dad for a visitation. My son's doctor finally said it was time for him to call child protection, and that I should again, too. I was terrified I would hear the words yet again, "You are doing everything you need to do protect your kids." This time, though, Child Family Services investigated the allegations from Nova Scotia and confirmed them. They told me in November 2018 to get another emergency protection order, which was granted. Child Family Services did an investigation. Thankfully, none of the kids disclosed anything, but the child welfare worker said it doesn't mean that if something did happen, they wouldn't disclose it at a later date.

My three-year-old was confused by her questions, and not answering properly—I could hear them through the door. I was nervous that something had happened, but that he didn't know how to tell us. Today, my son still says that when he was at his father's home, he hid from his daddy because he was scared. He's now four, and he has nightmares that his daddy is a monster and is going to kill him. He has not been with his dad for three months, but is only now becoming more vocal about his visits at his dad's. My worst fear now is that he will disclose something that happened.

I cannot tell you how grateful and proud I am of my predator's niece for finding the strength to come forward to help protect my son. I am also grateful to the others who are coming forward, and I know that this was not easy, nor will it be easy for any of them, as they go through the court process. I can say that I will be there to support them in any way I can. I will be there to give them a hug or to stand with them while they go through this process. I am grateful to the niece for responding to me that day in June, and allowing me to apologize to her for disregarding what she was trying to tell me earlier. Perhaps one day she will be able to tell her story to me, and I to her. I will never be able to thank her enough for trying to keep my son safe. That's all she wanted—to help one person keep their child safe from her predator.

In March of 2020, our predator was arrested at work by RCMP officers, and flown back to Nova Scotia to face twelve new child-related charges as a result of their investigation. As of the end of 2020, we are still waiting for his plea and a trial date, as Covid-19 has put a damper on the court processes.

Chapter Eleven

STRUGGLES

IT IS SUNDAY, February 10, 2019, late afternoon, and I am waiting for my next court date. I have tried to put my worries aside for the weekend so that I can relax. I was recently at the hospital again for the severe pain I have in my stomach since having pancreatitis. This happens a couple of times a month— the pain gets so bad that I have to go to a hospital to seek help. My family doctor has prescribed pain medication, but being in the battle of my life, I don't want to give my predator any way to be able to try to tell a Judge that I am an addict. So I take Advil or Tylenol. I also have toradol but it doesn't do much to ease the pain. Some days I just want to lie in bed and forget about the world. Some days I want to run away so that I can be sure that my kids will be safe.

Relaxing is so hard when all you can think about is what happens if...? With all the research I have done, I understood and was told that none of this would be easy. I researched why people don't come forward and don't go to the police when they have been sexually assaulted by a spouse. I get it now. I understand why, but I would not have changed one thing I have done so far to protect myself, my children, and his next possible victim. I will continue to fight to change the laws that protect my predator, laws that will make it easier to prosecute a spouse for sexual assault and easier to keep children safe from a parent who has suicidal tendencies and thoughts. I didn't have it in me to stay silent and let him sexually assault me and harass me and my children, and let him get away with it, only to turn around and have something worse happen to someone else.

Back in 2018 after leaving my predator I knew dealing with what happened to me would not be easy and so I sought help earlier on.. I was put on a very long waiting list after I called the Sexual Assault Center of Edmonton (SACE). I told a doctor at the hospital, who got me to speak to a social worker about what happened to me. The social worker managed to help my son and me for the few months I had to wait to see a therapist. I called another resource through Alberta Health Services. This also involved a wait, but at least I knew I would have help soon. I also contacted a self-care and wellness center. Their wait list was slightly shorter, and this is where I started.

In July of 2018, I went to my first session at the Wellness center. I couldn't hold back the tears anymore. I had contained, and not really released, the last few months of stress and anxiety. It felt like the world was sitting on my chest; I hid my face in my shirt, brought my knees up to my chest, and I cried. I cried listening to the music they played before our group session had started, and from listening to the other's stories, and how it related to my own. By the end of the session, my anxiety had lessened a teeny bit. I continued this therapy for a bit before my health declined. I hoped to return someday, as it was really beneficial.

With each new court date and each new Judge, my anxiety worsened. Having to tell every single Judge what happened to me over and over again was hard because my predator was always there to face me, to tell the Judge I was lying. That it didn't happen the way it sounded. My predator was getting mad that with each new charge he got, I was sure to tell the Judge about it. But how could I not? It was pertinent to what I was going through. What my kids had gone through. My predator chose not to stop. My predator chose not to listen to me, the police, my lawyers, or the Judges. This was his fault, and his alone. I didn't ask to be sexually assaulted daily. I didn't ask for further harassment and embarrassment, or to have my kids be involved in the chaos.

My health continues to decline, but I have faith every day that once the stress of this is all over, my body will be able to recover the way it should have when I was released from the hospital back in March of 2018. I live day by day. I don't eat much and have been diagnosed with functioning GI (which basically means the doctors have not a clue why I am still in so much pain), anorexia because I still cannot eat much, and the stress makes me eat less. I have neurological issues that are worrisome and see a neurologist on an ongoing basis, and I've been diagnosed with severe anxiety and posttraumatic stress disorder. I also have a sleeping disorder associated with the PTSD.

A big worry I have is that my body will fail after the stress is gone. It has been in "fight or flight" mode for a very long time. The body, I have come to realize, does not process trauma when we are still in "fight or flight." While talking to a therapist at SACE, we finally got into what my predator did to me. I had no problem sharing my story, but today was different. Today while sitting in that small room with my therapist, I didn't feel alone while talking about my predator and his actions. I could see him, and not the room I was sitting in. I could see my bed, and I could see him standing over me. I could feel him touching me, and I could smell him. It was the weirdest experience—I told my therapist that it was like I was somewhere else... back in that room with him. She says this is why we need to process trauma. This is what trauma does.

I see therapists regularly and have a massive support system from friends and family. If I can recommend to anyone going through this, take all the support you can get. Ask questions, google questions and answers. Not every person you speak to will be helpful. You may hit a few road blocks, but don't give up. I could not give up on my kids... but I also could not give up on myself. I wasn't told where I could go for help—I made the calls, I googled help centers. This is why I am writing this book. I feel there is a massive step missing between someone filing a statement, and receiving help. I didn't have anyone from victim services contact me until my predator was finally arrested for criminal harassment. I never had anyone call me from domestic violence services until my predator was arrested. I told as many authority figures as I could what happened to me, because I didn't want it to disappear. I didn't want to forget. I didn't want it to happen again. I spoke up.

I still fight today. Some days are harder than others, but my family and friends keep me in check between therapy and doctor's appointments. I think they just know when I am feeling down. I get more calls, daily check-ins, and lunch or dinner dates—meeting in Red Deer. All these things have helped me cope. To stay strong for my kids for myself. These people are my world and I need them more than ever.

My kids have been very vocal with their teachers about how they are feeling and what they have gone through, and I encourage them to keep talking it out. The school is even going to have my children talk to their counsellor, and my four-year-old is now finally, after five months on a waiting list, going to CASA (Child, Adolescent, and Family Mental Health). Unfortunately, I needed my predator's permission and signature to put our son in counselling and before CASA would help him. I didn't believe that my predator would give me permission to have our son in counselling and I surely did not think he would sign the paperwork to do so without a judge ordering him to do so. I will keep fighting for him, though. He will need the help.

Without the proper supports, I truly believe I would not be here today. This is not easy, but more people need to come forward so that it can get easier. There are flaws in the justice system, but as long as you do everything the way you're supposed to, things do work in your favour. Is it scary? Of course. Is it going to make you less stressed? No, probably not. But having a lawyer who believes you, having help from victims' services, who will come and sit with you in a courtroom to support you, walk you to your vehicle, help keep you safe, and help keep your predator away helps. Also having backup from the police and the Judges. All these things take time, and by God, I am the most patient person ever, but like I said before, the worst part about all of this has been the waiting. The not knowing. I fear seeing my predator in court each time, but it will not stop me from showing up. It will not stop me from telling the truth.

I am so ready to face my predator in court at his trial in June. I am ready to tell the Judge and anyone else in that room what my predator did to my kids and I for months. I want to tell my story. I want to be heard. I don't want to be silenced by this monster. I won't be. After all of this is over for me and I know that my mental health has healed my goal is to help others going through this. My goal is to work with the Domestic Violence Unit with the Edmonton Police so I can help others like me. Help them find the resources I had to find myself. Have someone they can talk to. Support them the way I have been supported by so many people. I want others to tell their story and for them to have asafe place to tell it. I want to one day be able to stand together to end domestic violence and the stigma that it's hard to have a spouse prosecuted for sexually assaulting or abusing you.

I am just one person. People say I am strong. That they admire my strength. I went from saying I was a fighter to being told I was a warrior. I still don't know how I feel about being told I am strong. Some days I don't feel strong, but I sure try to be for my kids and for myself. I don't have to be, but I want to be. So I guess I am strong. I am a warrior. I can do this. You can, too.

The days leading up to a court date are my most anxious days. One, because I have to remind myself I have done everything I can to protect my children and myself. Two, because I ca not control what will happen or not happen in a courtroom. I cannot make the decision for a Judge; I can only hope that the Judge, when he meets me and has read my affidavit, believes what I am telling him, and believes that my family is at risk from my predator. Three, I never know what to expect of my predator. What his thoughts are, what his next move is, and of course the big one, having to see his smirking face.

Every court session is different. With a protection order, I saw a different Judge every time. In the family court process, it's the same, except in certain circumstances, a Judge can say, "One court, One Judge." I have yet to run into this, but I did hear it today at court. When things get complicated and costly, not only for the parties involved, but also for the court system itself. I want one court, one Judge. At least then that one person will know every single thing I have gone through, and I will be able to stop explaining it to every new Judge.

Today was another anxious day. Last night I got very little sleep, and by the time I arrived at court, I had a massive migraine. I received an email from my lawyer; she sounded like she was giving up just before the weekend. She told me that unless something new has come up, I needed to prepare for my predator to have unsupervised visits again. I was firm with my response—I told my lawyer that I had not fought this hard to keep my child safe to just give up now. I was not going to let my predator have access to my child without supervision, and most certainly not to do exchanges at the daycare, which is what he was asking for. I said, "Absolutely not! I just moved and had to relocate to hide from this predator, and he wants to exchange at the daycare, with no one to watch his every move and keep us safe. Nope, not even a question. It's just not happening." My lawyer said "okay."

I learned today that when it comes to my children, I am their voice, to keep them safe. I had to stand up for what I believed was in their best interest right now. My victim services support person asked me what I wanted when I got a last-minute email from my lawyer, basically saying, "Come up with a plan B, in case things head south." I told my victim services support person that the most I am willing to give him is supervised visitation until this new investigation for the other allegations is complete. She said, "Then tell your lawyer that. Tell her you're not backing down."

The scariest thing in the world is something happening to our children, and not knowing if we have done everything we could have done to protect them. I know I have literally taken every right step to ensure my children's safety, but as a mother, it still doesn't seem like enough when you feel your child is at risk. Your worries don't become less when people tell you that you've done everything you can, and it's out of your hands and in the hands of a Judge.

It is February 12, 2019. I had court this morning to see if I could get a parenting order that asked that my predator have supervised visitation with my four-year-old son. I know that he will in some way have access to my son; I just believe that, right now, supervised visitation is safest. I went to the court house feeling my stomach turn, I had a lump in my throat, and I felt like I was going to throw up. As always, I looked around anxiously to make sure my predator was nowhere near me.

To my surprise, the officer who once showed up before did so again. Again, he was not obligated to, but his support was extremely appreciated! My victim services support person and I were chatting about what I was going to tell my lawyer. I asked the officer what he thought. He also believed that, right now, supervised visitation was best. When my lawyer arrived, she wanted me to tell her my plan B. I didn't have one. She said we have to try to have the upper hand. If we make a deal with my predator right now, we may have a shot. Once I told my lawyer what I was willing to work with, she went and got my predator. She pulled him out of the courtroom to speak to him while the officer, my victim services support person, and I sat about twenty feet away.

I couldn't handle him looking at me so I got up and went to the washroom. I took the long way so that I didn't have to walk by my predator. When I came back, my lawyer was just finishing up her conversation with him. When she came back, I was very surprised to hear that he had consented to supervised visits, at his cost. I was in shock. I felt like someone was watching over us. Perhaps it was the officer's presence again that made him see the seriousness of my asking for supervised visits. I don't know what it was, but I was so grateful. The officer did not need to come into the courtroom this time. He did, however, wait till we were done, to walk us back to our vehicles.

I can't stress enough how much support helps when you have to repeatedly go back and forth to court. To continuously face your abuser. To not know what will happen in a court room, and which way a Judge will sway with his or her decision. My lawyer was only trying to give me realistic outcomes, but it stressed me out more. This was not my lawyer's fault because, as a lawyer, her job is to give me an idea of all scenarios and outcomes. They honestly have no idea which way a Judge will sway, either.

Today I took as a win. Today I got to keep my baby safe for a little while longer. Today I am proud I stood my ground. Today I am grateful for the support of all those who were thinking of us, or who were with me. Now I wait until my next court date of March 1, 2019 for the second oral hearing for the emergency protection order.

Chapter Twelve

FINALLY SAFE

AFTER WAITING SEVERAL more days, today my predator and I were back in court for the oral hearing of the Emergency Protection Order. The days leading up to this were exhausting, overwhelming, and full of anxiety. Something I never saw myself doing was praying to God, and praying so much! Now that the allegations were out in the open, this Emergency Protection Order had to stay in place. Again, I asked the same officer to come to my defense, and the same victim services worker told me she would be there, too. My lawyer didn't sound extremely hopeful that this Emergency Protection Order would stick. The whole reason for having the order was to protect my children, an order that Child Family Services insisted I get.

The problem, my lawyer thought, was that Child Family Services had opened an assessment and investigated my three children, as well as my predator's two children, and thankfully none of the children disclosed anything. My four-year-old son was still struggling with something, though. I still had reasonable fear for his safety, and my own. After Child Family Services closed their assessment, I was left on my own to ensure the Emergency Protection Order stayed in place. I guess to them, me fighting on my own to protect my son was protection enough for him. This frustrated me and my lawyers. It was now my predator's word against my own. Not having a Child Family Services worker come to court and speak to a Judge on behalf of my son left so many things up in the air.

Another thing my lawyer thought would catch the Judge's attention was that I already had two orders that specified No contact. One was from my predator's arrest back in August 2018, bail conditions that prevented him from direct or indirect contact with neither my son or me, except in the case of a parenting order that had been granted by the Court of Queens Bench. The second was a restraining order. This order also was to prevent my predator from contacting me directly or indirectly, but this one did not include my children. My lawyer thought the Judge would see that these orders already existed, and she would vacate the Emergency Protection Order. Judges do not usually stack up protection orders. This left my mind wandering again, before court, about the "what happens if…?" "How can I protect my son if…?"

That's all I have wanted. To protect my children. Knowing the allegations that came forward from my predator's niece scared me to death; I really didn't want leave my sweet tiny four-year-old alone with his father. If something had not actually happened yet, to me it felt like it was only a matter of time before something did. Will the stress of my predator knowing he will be arrested again turn into a situation where, if he can't have our son, neither can I? Will the stress and fear of this arrest to come make my predator take my four-year-old and run? There have been so many news reports lately of ex-spouses taking the children, and the children end up dying. I couldn't fathom these thoughts. All I knew was I had to keep trying. I had to keep fighting for my son's safety.

Today is March 1, 2019. At 9 a.m. I arrived at the courthouse and waited for my victim services worker. I was completely calm. I am not sure why I was calm and not anxious like every other court date prior, except I had a dream the night before showing me things would be okay and when I woke up I was calm. I had no anxiety, no stress, and no worries. It felt peaceful. I felt like today was going to be okay. Today I was to face my predator in a courtroom and tell the Judge why I had legitimate fear for my safety and that of my children, and why the Emergency Protection Order needed to stay in place. My victim services worker and I arrived at the courtroom and sat outside. I could see my predator sitting behind a low tree in the waiting area. I pointed him out to the victim services worker. She immediately said, "Well, that's pretty creepy." She and I sat and chatted while waiting for my lawyer. Usually we would talk about how I was feeling before going in. Even knowing that today my predator could ask me questions of his own as he represented himself, I wasn't worried. Not because I was feeling cocky, but because I really felt like things were going to work out. Today we talked about the book I was writing, how my kids were doing, and about the doctor's appointment I had just had the previous day.

My lawyer was running late and apologized. I told her it was okay. It was time for us to head into the courtroom. I still had not felt any anxiety. The cases before ours where each party consented to orders went first. After those had finished, my lawyer stood up. The last Judge had allowed two hours for our hearing today. This Judge seemed fair. My lawyer went up and started to speak to the Judge. Being brutally honest, she said, "Yes, there are already two other orders in place, but we are insisting that Emergency Protection Order also stay in place." My lawyer brought up the Criminal Harassment charges, and the trial date for those charges—she knew that every Judge and lawyer knows that a criminal harassment charge that goes through to a trial is big. My predator nodded his head up and down in agreement to the charges and trial date. My lawyer then told the Judge that my predator and I were to be back in court March 4, 2019 to have the parenting order revised, something that still had not been done because my predator kept putting it off, and adjourning it. During the previous court date, he had agreed under non-prejudice to have supervised visitation that was to be set up by him, and paid for by him. To date, nothing has been set up. The Judge heard every word. She then said she would have wanted to hear directly from Child Family Services, but of course they were not there. They deemed their job complete. The Judge told my predator that she was keeping the Emergency Protection Order in place until October 31, 2019. This overlapped the date the restraining order expires. This order was renewable should I need to renew it after it expired.

My predator was not happy. He asked the Judge why the order needed to stay in place. If the order was granted because of the allegations, he wanted to be clear that he didn't agree with the allegations. The Judge told him she would write on the Emergency Protection Order that he did not agree with the allegations, but that the order was to stay in place until October 31, 2019, and he needed to make sure he showed up to his next court date and hand in an affidavit. He told the judge that he had handed in his affidavit that morning. My predator immediately left the courtroom. This is something he rarely did so I knew he was mad.

The officer had tried to come but got tied up at work with something more pressing. But he did look into whether or not the warrants had been put out for my predator's arrest. They had not been done yet. It was extremely painful for me to sit back and wait. I think my officer felt the same. He was relieved to know that the Emergency Protection Order remained in place. He was going to try to come to my next court date, which was Monday. Today was a win!

Another weekend of wonder and worry. Again, I was praying to God that the next Judge would change the parenting order after hearing and understanding my fears for my son's safety, as well as my own. I did not hear from my family law lawyer on Friday. I knew this was going to be out of both our hands. I tried to think positive—if I were a Judge and there were all these protection orders in place, what would I do. If it involved a child, I did not know. The Judge had to try to be reasonable and understanding to both parties. As much as I knew I had to keep my son safe, I also knew that this could be the biggest life changing event in his short little life thus far. My four-year-old had not had any sort of contact with his dad since November 13, 2018. My son no longer thinks he even has a sister. I reassure him he does, and that he will one day be able to see his sister and brother again. This is something that will have to be worked out later on.

On Monday March 4, 2019, I woke at 4 a.m. unable to sleep. I wasn't super anxious. I felt really awake and just unable to go back to sleep. Of course, I pondered what was to come of this day. Today was hopefully going to end the running back and forth to court; I hoped we would have a parenting order that allowed my predator only supervised visitation. I was also asking for sole decision-making, something I was unsure a Judge would allow. I prayed hard, hoping that having the Emergency Protection Order that past Friday would show the Judge how dire this situation was. At seven o'clock I woke my three boys. I fed them breakfast and got my older one off to school, my four-year-old off to daycare, and my middle one to his dad's, because he was ill. I arrived at court a little later than I wanted to because the traffic was exceptionally heavy. I took my time as I had left myself plenty of extra time. Again today, I was not super anxious. Maybe slightly more than Friday, but nothing like I had been in the past. I didn't have the same fear of my predator anymore. I could see him wearing down and wearing out. I could see that his fight was making him lose focus. My focus stayed on my son. I met my victim services workers at the courthouse, and waited in their office until almost ten o'clock. One of them, I had not been in contact with since January, and she told me I looked so much more relaxed about today. She said she could see that my body language had also changed. I told her, "I have done everything I can. I can do nothing more than what I have done to try to ensure my son's safety. It is literally out of my hands, and in the hands of a stranger. She seemed proud of my strength. I told her about my two-year plan, and all the things I planned to accomplish within those two years. She was impressed.

At about ten minutes to ten, we walked to the other side of the courthouse on the Court of Queens Bench side. We made our way up to the third floor and headed straight into the courtroom, and waited for my lawyer to arrive; she was running a bit behind. I was not worried. My case was number twenty-one on the list for the day. I was able to listen to the Judge a little bit with other cases to get a sense of her fairness. For the parties ahead of ours, she allowed both parties to speak and listened to both sides. By listening to rule on other parenting orders, she did seem fair, but also hard to read. My victim services worker was worried. My lawyer showed up at about ten after ten. She pulled us out, and into the little quiet room just outside the courtroom to see what I was asking for. I told her I want him to have supervised visits, and at his expense. For all he had put my kids and me through over the last year, that did not seem unreasonable to me. I told her I wanted my four-year-old to go to therapy, and I wanted to ask the Judge to either make him sign the papers that I had brought for CASA, or to allow me sole decision-making. For my lawyer and me, that seemed the most logical, and was in the best interest of my son. She asked how he could contact me, so I would know where and when to bring our son for his visitations. Up to this point, he had had no contact with my family. They ended that very early on. I spoke to my mom while sitting with my lawyer to see if he could email her with the facility name, the time I was to bring our son, and on what dates. Nothing more. She agreed. After going into the courtroom and speaking to my predator she came back and told me my predator, of course, did not agree to email my mom. He was more comfortable messaging my sister. I didn't have time to ask my sister but knew she would be fine helping me if she could. It was finally our turn before the Judge. I did not need to go and stand before the Judge. My lawyer told me to sit in the gallery. My predator represented himself, so he stood before the Judge.

My lawyer started by explaining to the Judge why I was seeking Supervised visits. She said that there were three protection orders in place, and the last one was confirmed on Friday. She told the judge that my predator was charged with criminal harassment, obstruction of justice, and publication of intimate photos online without permission. She explained to the Judge that the harassment did not stop after his arrest, and that my predator continued to follow me from the police station part way home before veering off.

The Judge then allowed my predator to speak. He told the Judge why he thought I got the Emergency Protection Order. He lied to the Judge. He told her it was only for the things my son was saying, and what I reported to my son's doctor, who then called

Child Family Services to get them involved. He then told the Judge that at the Emergency Protection Hearing, the Judge wrote on the Emergency Protection Order that Child Family Services had closed their file, and that he did not agree with the allegations.

The Judge then asked him if the Emergency Protection Order was confirmed. My predator replied yes. She then asked him, why if there was nothing wrong, a Judge who had evidence from both parties, myself and my predator, then chose to keep the order in place, even knowing there were two other orders already. My predator again told the Judge that he did not know and that he didn't agree with it. The Judge told him, "Well, it's in place for a reason." My predator then lied again, telling the Judge that after his arrest nothing further happened—he said he wasn't stalking and harassing me further, past September. Again the Judge said, "But there is an Emergency Protection Order in place, and it wouldn't be in place if the claimant (me) had not been scared for her safety, and that of the children." I could see the frustration in my predator's face. I was worried about what the Judge would say next.

My lawyer stood up and addressed the sole decision-making decision that I was seeking. She explained to the Judge that my predator did not want to allow our son to go to therapy. That he didn't need it. He tried to tell the Judge while sitting down that he felt it was not in the best interest that our son to go to therapy. The Judge cut him off, and told him that when he was speaking to her, that he needed to be standing up. Again he shook his head, but did as she asked. The Judge said, "I don't understand why you would not want him to have therapy. The mother would not be asking if she didn't feel he needed it." My predator again lied (I know, shocking...) telling the Judge this was the first time he had heard about me wanting our son to go to therapy, when in fact, he had known since Sept 2018. My lawyer was sure to explain that to the Judge. I could feel my fingers numbing as I squeezed my hands together tightly in anticipation, dodging my head around my lawyer so that I could look directly at the Judge. My victim services worker was nervous for me, thinking things were not looking good for us. I was becoming anxious. The next thing my lawyer brought up were the allegations from Nova Scotia, and the pending charges that had not yet been laid for child molestation. The Judge asked if it was in regards to my son. My lawyer said no.

My heart pounded. I felt like I was going to throw up. The hardest part was reminding myself not to speak unless spoken to. To make sure I didn't screw up and say something that would hurt my case and risk my son's safety. Listening to the lies was the hardest thing I have had to do so far, biting my tongue and learning that my lawyer would in fact stand up for me and advocate on my behalf. This was the first real fight in court we had. The majority of the other court dates had been pushed off for months. My lawyer wanted it to end today for me. My predator told the Judge he could not afford supervised visits because he was paying an excessive amount of child support payments and spousal to his ex-wife. He told the Judge he was working at having the payments lowered so it was more affordable and fairer. All I could think was that, over the last several years, he didn't fight to have those payments lowered, and I didn't believe he was even trying now. The Judge basically told him: too bad. That this court session was about visiting his son and not about his other obligations.

Thankfully, the Judge saw through all his lies. She granted him supervised visits at his own cost through a third-party facility, and granted me sole decision-making for our son. I cannot even explain how I felt, hearing those words. My body shook involuntarily. Maybe from shock, maybe the stress had finally released, or maybe some adrenaline, too. I was on the verge of happy tears, but I was able to hold myself together. My predator was beyond livid. I am pretty sure I got the glare of death as he left the courtroom. I then looked at my victim services worker, and said, "Let me guess—this is where I really need to watch my back." She shook her head up and down to say yes. After my lawyer gathered up her things, the three of us quietly left the courtroom. In the lobby, I could not hold in the excitement and relief I felt. I asked my lawyer if it would be inappropriate to give her a hug. She looked at me with a small grin, and said not at all. We had both been on this long court journey. She had fought this battle with me, for me. Another win. My kid was finally safe. Right now, my predator had no a clue that we had moved, or where. Right now, I am off the ground floor, and for the first time, I feel like I could leave my patio door open in the summer, and not worry that he will bust through it. Although I know I still need to be very careful and aware of my surroundings, I feel semi-safe for the first time in almost a year. My kids finally feel safe.

Chapter Thirteen

THE OUTCOME

I HAD TAKEN a short break from writing while I waited for the trial date. My anxiety was getting the best of me again. My emotions had taken over my body. I cried on a dime; I would cry for hours. I was so angry that I was crying, because I couldn't figure out why my emotions suddenly decided to come to the surface. The more I cried, the more frustrated and angry I became. It was becoming so bad that I was beginning to think that not waking up at all would be better than dealing with all of this. I was beginning to push everyone out, to push them all away. I just wanted to...not be here anymore, but I also realized that I could not leave my children. It was tearing me apart from the inside out—the anxiety of the trial, the anxiety I knew I was going to feel telling strangers and yet another Judge what happened to me in the last year and a bit, and stress about the outcome of the trial.

I met with my Victim Services worker, and she assured me what I was feeling was absolutely normal. That my body was on its last legs. She said, "Think of it this way, your body for the last year and bit has been constantly in fight or flight. The trial is the final stage to end everything that has happened. It's closure." My body was not tolerating this well, I felt betrayed by my own body as I continued to fight through the tears each and every day.

On May 10, 2019, I received a call from the crown prosecutor's assistant telling me that I no longer needed to meet with them on May 21, 2019 to go over everything that would be brought up in the trial. My predator had decided to plead guilty two weeks before the trial date. I was confused and thought perhaps he was offered a plea deal but, up until this point I had not heard about any plea deals from the crown. After speaking to the crown prosecutor they told me they did not offer him any deals and said he was pleading guilty on his own.. On May 22, 2019, at around 10 a.m. I heard my predator's defense lawyer tell the judge he was pleading guilty to the charges of Criminal Harassment. I had four people sitting with me as I listened to the crown explain to the Judge what had occurred over the last year and why there was a criminal harassment charge. Thankfully this Judge did not seem to take any crap. The Judge asked my predator if he realized he was pleading guilty to a very serious offence, my predator's response, a simple "Ya." My predator came in unshaven, wearing cargo pants and a black sweater. He looked like he didn't have a care in the world. This was the first time I had really looked at him since I left him last April. Walking into the courtroom, I could see him smirk, and I think the Judge did, too.

The Judge asked the crown if they wanted to make any changes to my predator's current bail conditions as my predator was going to be on bail until his sentencing date. The crown replied, "He would like to have his phone back so he can FaceTime with his son." All I could think, while I shook so badly was, "Holy crap! He lied to the Judge. He didn't tell his lawyer about the new Emergency protection order or about the newest parenting order." The Judge immediately said, "No, I will not be giving him his phone back. Actually, what I am considering doing is removing any electronics, including his computer, Xbox or PlayStation, or anything that could connect to the Internet from his home." I watched my mom's hands release from the bench in front of us. I was shaking so much. The judge went on to ask the defense lawyer if he wanted to request anything. The lawyer said, "Well your honor, my client will get his phone back sooner or later; why not now? The Judge's response was, "You're right, but not today."

I gave a small sigh of relief, and I had a feeling of faith in this Judge. The Judge then told my predator that if he even made the slightest error in breach of his bail conditions, he would end up back in his courtroom in front of him. He told him that he basically owned him until July 24, 2019 at 1:30 in the afternoon when he would be sentenced by this very Judge. I had so many mixed feelings about him pleading guilty. I knew he would have the likelihood of a lighter sentence; I wanted him to be in jail, not on probation, where he could potentially come after me in retaliation; and also because I still feared this monster.

The crown called me afterwards to tell me they were considering probation because technically this is his "first" offence, and they were even considering a pardon. I fought! I told them there were new protection orders that were just put through in March, there was a new parenting order in place, and he was very aware of this order that did not allow him to FaceTime with his son, and there was a new police report on his constant stalking, after his arrest in August all the way up to mid-November.

Then I had to wait until the sentencing date on July 24, 2019 to meet with the crown prosecutor so I could give them my input, but it seemed to me that it won't matter, as they will do what they need to do. I just pray that this Judge does not just let my predator walk out of that courtroom in July.

While waiting for the sentencing, I kept busy. I joined a domestic violence therapy group held by Family Services. It is a seven-week course that has been really good. Being with others and hearing about their fights has helped me a little. It's a safe place for us to go and be real, to talk about whatever we have gone through, and not be judged by anyone who has not gone through this themselves. My victim services worker set me up with this group. There have been so many great resources that I have had the privilege to work with, including the John Howard Society, Victim Services through the court provided service the Domestic Violence Complaint Assistance Program DVCAP, Family Services, and Kids Kottage (I have yet to take my children here, but I will use them when things settle down). There is also the Elizabeth Fry Society of Edmonton, the Edmonton Mental Health Clinic, the Soluna Wellness Center, and the Sexual Assault Center of Edmonton—so many resources, including a few I have yet to look into. I highly recommend looking in your city and province for resources like these to help you out. You can start by asking your local police victim services unit for resources to start with. You will get more resources, the more people you come into contact with.

I understand that it is hard to talk about what has happened to us; I get that people just want it to go away and hope it's forgotten. But what happens when, down the road, you're triggered? You haven't dealt with your trauma, and suddenly a mass of memories and senses come flooding back? If I can recommend any one thing, find your resource so you can get help. Take care of yourself so that you can take care of your family. Dealing with court is not easy, but it is possible when you have the support you need sitting by your side. There are people out there who want to help you, not to force you to go to the police and file a report, nor to get you to stand in front of a Judge and be forced to get protection orders. They are there to help you through everything and anything you may need. If you are worried about finances, most of these are free to use; some have time limits, but there are so many resources it's hard to run out of help, assistance, and guidance.

This has not been an easy battle. Fighting for my kids' safety, for my safety, and every single court session—both criminal court and family court—but if I had to file a report with the police all over again, I would not change a thing about how I handled this whole situation. I did everything I should have, and I did it correctly. Sometimes it works out well for the victim, and sometimes it does not. Luck was on my side, but I also never gave up.

Today is July 8, 2019, I am sitting on an airplane on my first vacation in almost six years. Last night I didn't sleep a wink; I felt anxious and full of guilt for leaving my children behind, and especially my four-year-old, who has become so attached to me since his visits with his dad stopped. I worry the most for him because he is so unsure in his little world, unable to understand why his father suddenly disappeared, but also scared the one constant in his life will leave, too, and may not come back.

I reassure him that I most certainly am coming back to my boy. I left a little calendar for him with pictures about what my trip will entail, a picture of a plane, a picture of where I am going, pictures of people I will see, and a picture of when I return to him. I hope this will give him some small peace of mind. I know he is in good hands; he has stayed with my sister and my friend before, but it's different this time.

On Valentine's day, my dad called to tell me he wanted to give me a gift. He said, "You never go anywhere, and you never buy things for yourself. I am heading down east (to Prince Edward Island) in the summer, and I would like to fly you out to meet me there, and come on the back of my motorcycle and ride through the Cabot Trail with me in Nova Scotia." I was humbled.

This is exactly what I needed after this year, and I think he knew it. I needed the break, the relaxation, the beautiful views, and the wind on my face— six days after I return home, I will hear my predator's fate.

My trip was amazing! I was so happy to see my brother and his family, my aunts and uncles, grandfather on Prince Edward Island and my best friend to spend time with them. My four-year-old did amazingly well, and he had so much fun with my sister and my friend. I came home to really big hugs and lots of love from all three boys telling me tales of their adventures while I was away. Cabot Trail was beautiful! The sights and scenery were astounding from the back of a motorcycle, something I realized right away would have been completely different in the back of a car, through a window. The fresh air on my face and the soothing motion of the bike around the corners made me wish it would last a little longer. There are so many pictures of this amazing trip—I will be forever grateful.

On July 24, 2019, at 11 a.m. in the morning I met with the crown prosecutor. Surrounding me was my mom, my sister, my two friends, and one of my victim services workers. I went in there dreading that I would hear, yet again, that they would not even ask for any type of real sentence. Boy, was I wrong! While on holidays, I got a call from a parole officer who was asked to write a pre-sentence report. She asked me if I was willing to speak with her about what happened to me. Of course I was! I knew that this pre-sentence report could have an impact on the sentencing, and I wanted the best possible results from the sentence that I could get. To my surprise, the crown had read the report. She told me that she had not made a final decision yet, but was now thinking of a more punitive sentence. I didn't want to get my hopes up, but she explained three options to me.

One, three years' probation; two, probation with a fine; and three, jail and probation. I told her that if she seeks a fine, he won't pay it. He hasn't paid me a dime, and he is in mounds of debt—she found that helpful to know. I told her that I didn't expect a huge jail sentence, but something would be better than nothing. I said two months, four months, even six months, and she told me she was thinking of thirty days in jail, and the rest probation. I told her that this meant thirty days of my kids and myself feeling safe, really safe, for the first time in over a year. I hoped this would weigh heavily in the outcome. I was disappointed to learn that the defense lawyer came in asking for an adjournment. I really thought this would all be over; now I have to wait a few more months for another sentencing date. I remained hopeful, though.

I received a call from the crown prosecutor's assistant while I was waiting to go into my appointment at the Sexual Assault Center. She told me that sentencing had been put off until December 13, 2019. The tears immediately flowed down my cheeks as I tried to ask, "Why? How? How does he get to continue to walk the streets while I have to hide?" I was exhausted, overwhelmed with fear all over again, and overwhelmed with emotion.

Thankfully I was at my scheduled appointment when she called. I needed to be there. I had thoughts that, to me, were the most peaceful thoughts I have had in a while, and they terrified me. I was sitting in the tub having a bath when all I could think was how relaxing it would be to slice my wrists and watch the blood flow; how peaceful it would be to slowly drift off to sleep.

I knew this was wrong, which is why I was so terrified. I had no idea what it meant to think these thoughts. I had no idea what made it seem so peaceful. It was a lot.

December 13, 2019 could not come soon enough. I was scared, but also ready for this day to come. As I walked into the courtroom with my mom, my sister, my friend, and my victim services worker, the crown Prosecutor approached me. She brought me in between the doors, as my predator was already at the defense table with his lawyer. The crown Prosecutor explained to me that she was going to be asking the Judge for jail time. She was looking for anything between one day and ninety days, something she said the Judge would decide. I felt some small amount of relief.

After we had spoken, we walked into the courtroom and sat down behind the crown's desk. As the court clerk announced the Judge's entry, we were asked to stand. When the Judge said, "Good morning; please sit," I was on the edge of my seat, my legs shaking badly. The crown had asked me if I would like to read my victim impact statement, and I told her I did. I needed to. The Judge called for a recess so that he could go over the pre-sentence report and my three victim impact statements. I chose to read the last one I wrote. The crown and defense had to go over my statement before it was read so that I was only reading and saying facts that were proven in my predator's guilty plea. It took a half hour. It felt much longer.

Finally, everyone returned to the courtroom, I was asked to approach the crown's desk so that I could read my impact statement. Before going to court, my mom told me to be strong, to not show any weakness. As I started to read my statement, I was so angry. I was so angry that I did shed some tears, but out of anger for being made to be quiet, for being scared, for him scaring my children. I had the right to be pissed right off with this man—he claimed he loved us all, but then he hurt us all.

Here is what I said to the Judge, to the the crown, to the defense, and to the monster who sat there, I could tell he was scared shitless because of the way he sat. He had his shoulders slumped over, his head down never looking up as he finally felt defeated, he never looked away from the top of the desk that sat in front of him and I could see him nervously playing with his hands in his lap. He didn't know what was going to happen to him.

Victim Impact Statement #3
Nov 20, 2019

It has been 492 days since you were arrested, and 594 days since I left you because of domestic violence. 594 days of living in fear of you, 594 days of living in fight or flight, 594 days that I had very little sleep, 594 days of trying to explain to my young children why you wanted us to fear you, and why you were hurting us. 594 days where my health has declined, 594 days my parents worried for my life, and 594 days my children and I can never get back. You stole my sense of safety, and you stole a part of my life because of your constant harassment, your possessive and obsessive behaviour, and because I chose to protect my children and myself by going to the police to file a report, and to get protection orders.

I left with the little strength I had after being hospitalized for 46 long days due to pancreatitis from a complication in a procedure. I was on a feeding tube, and even after I was released, I had to go back multiple times due to severe weakness and a heart that would beat so fast it felt as though it would pop out of my chest. You then built an entire public Facebook page that had my name, my pictures, and my children's pictures all over it, trying to work around the restraining order, in another fashion to contact me. Again, you wouldn't let up saying that you loved me, that you would never give up on "us," that you couldn't see me with anyone else, and therefore again threatened suicide. You then chose to post very private and intimate photos of me online from a boudoir session we had done together in private. To say this surprised me, hurt me, and embarrassed me, is to say the least. You tried to steal my dignity, making these images public to my family, to my friends, and to my work.

There has been no real remorse for what you have done; you don't feel you are in the wrong, only that you were the one wronged.

594 days so far of living in fear, 594 days of living with PTSD from the trauma I have endured, 594 days of doctors and specialists, not knowing why my body is not recovering and getting better; instead my health is declining. This has left the doctors uncertain what my outcome will be. 594 days, and I had to uproot my children, not once, but twice. I did not have the finances to move right away, so my children and I bounced back and fourth between friend's and family's homes till I was able to find another place to live; my children had to miss a bunch of school while we bounced around. For 594 days, I have had to look over my shoulder, wondering if you were there behind me, following me, going to grab me, going to stab me, going to kill me. 594 days I thought I was going to end up in a body bag, trying to explain to my children—should something happen to their mommy make sure to call 9-1-1 and run. I should not have had to prepare my children for anything like this! My children should not have had to fear you because you could not control yourself.

I had to face you several times in court, scared, sick to my stomach, shaking uncontrollably. I have constant nightmares that you have broken into my home, of you following us, of my assault. I am on numerous medications for my conditions including an antidepressant and sleeping aid, as well as anti-anxiety meds because I can no longer hold a conversation with anyone while looking directly at them; I no longer trust people, I no longer feel safe to be in an elevator with a man alone, I no longer feel safe to walk alone anywhere. I rarely leave my home unless I have an appointment, or I am with my family. I have had to speak to my children's school about a safety plan should you ever try to show up there; I have had to speak to their daycare; I have to be cautious in every aspect of my life because I still fear you, because I still fear you are not done with me, that you will retaliate because I went to the police for help. The trauma caused by your actions will go beyond these 594 days for myself and for my children.

My fear is that you will walk out of here today thinking you didn't get punished, and that you will wait a short time before starting all over again with me. I will always have to watch my back; I will always have to make sure my kids know our safety plan; I will always fear for my life and my safety, and for those around me who support me. Financially you drove me into the ground, moving twice, paying to restart our lives fresh, through court, leaving me with our old house bills, and for the last year solely supporting our son. It has never ended, and I feel it won't end regardless of the outcome today. You kept telling me I never had to fear you, that you would never hurt me, that you loved me. You did hurt me, you hurt our children, you abandoned your son, you made me fearful of you, you made me fear for my life, and you made me fearful in every single aspect in my life, with how I do things now. This will affect my future relationships because of not knowing if I will be hurt in the same manner, if I can trust them to be with my children alone, if I will be stalked, harassed, and getting three hundred unwanted messages a day.

I will end with this: a reminder that I have had to fear for my life, my safety, and my children's safety for the last 594 days. I have had insurmountable stress, anxiety, PTSD, and fear, living a life of fight or flight which has taken a massive hit on my health and recovery in a long illness. I will have to continue therapy, I will have to continue watching my back, protecting my children, fearing for our lives, and our safety, should you walk out of here today. I want to feel safe again, I want my kids to feel safe again, I want our lives back. We deserve to feel safe again.

You tried to silence me; I will no longer be silent. I will for the rest of my life help those who lost their voices to people like you!

I could hear my mom crying behind me, my sister sobbing, and my friend consoling. I could see the Judge wipe his eyes, the crown needing Kleenex, and my predator avoiding any sort of eye contact. Perhaps if he had looked at me, he would have actually had real remorse? Perhaps he couldn't handle the fact that my tears were real.

The Judge thanked me for coming in, for my heartfelt statement, and said he was proud of me for having the strength to come in and speak. He then asked me to go and sit back down by my family. My mom, still crying. grabbed me and hugged me tight. I was vibrating, holding my mom's hand, probably a little too tight, but not knowing I was doing so.

The Judge then spoke to the defense. The defense said that what my predator had done to me is not as bad as a file he had found in Saskatchewan; he even had it printed out, and he gave it to the Judge. From what I remember, the Judge quickly glanced at it and then pushed it aside. Next, the defense gave the Judge a letter from my predator's work, to say he was doing well at his job, that he was in management, and that my predator had no interest in going back to school which was good because then he could not use that as an excuse to not go to jail. The Judge looked at the letter and asked when it was written, as it had no date. A mistake on the defense's side.

Next, my predator was allowed to speak. The Judge cautioned him, saying that he did not need to hear from my predator, but that he had to give him the chance to speak. My predator tried to force tears out, blaming everything he did to us on the fact that he was sad. He said that I broke his heart when I left him, that he didn't cope well, and that he was in counselling, but that his therapist wouldn't write a letter for him. He told the Judge that he also hurt his other two children, and they would also need counselling. He ended with an uncaring apology, not once looking at the Judge or myself.

After my predator said his piece, the Judge was ready to determine his sentence. He told my predator that he was lucky to have a good lawyer; he told my predator that if he did love me, then he would not have posted those intimate photos of me online publicly to hurt me, but that he would instead have posted a picture "...of say, her having a picnic?" He told my predator that he was going to make him an example for younger generations so that they understand that when you break up with someone, stalking and harassing them is not the route to go.

I froze. I stopped breathing. I waited. The Judge finally said, "You will be sentenced to 45 days in jail to be served intermittently." I let out a huge sigh, and cried. Relief! I did it. I made it to the end, I faced my predator, I hopefully stopped it from happening again. I did not hear the rest of what the Judge ordered, but I later found out he also has two years' probation, with extensive probation orders to follow. All this to say, my predator will be busy for the next five months, every single weekend. My kids and I will get some relief. Some sense of safety. Finally.

Chapter Fourteen.

BELIEF

I THINK ONE of my biggest fears about coming forward to my friends and family was that I would feel unheard, not believed, and judged harshly for allowing my predator to abuse me for so long because I didn't know it was happening. No one wants to disappoint their family. I will say I am very much a family-oriented person. The feeling of letting them down was, to me, one of the worst parts about this whole thing. The first person to really listen to me was my friend. I went to her house the day after I was sexually assaulted. I told her what happened. She wanted to keep me safe. She told me of her past experience with an abuser. I felt bad for her. I was still uncertain about what had happened to me. I just knew I was terrified to be alone with my predator. That I didn't trust him anymore and had this gut feeling that it was only going to get worse.

Next, my best friend of twenty years, down east. I messaged her while at my friend's house, asking for her advice. Any advice. I was so scared of what people were going to think; so scared they would think I was just going crazy. She believed me, too. She was also the one to contact my sister. My sister called as soon as she got off the phone with my best friend. She begged me to leave that night. She told me I was not safe. In my gut, I knew she was right, but I was so scared of my predator waiting for me to come home, missing work the next day, trying to find me, that I felt it was best I go home until I could figure out what was happening. I told my sister not to tell my parents what was happening, or what had happened; I didn't want them to know yet. She agreed not to say anything. My sister was one of the people who stood with me at the sentencing, and I was so glad to have her there.

Next was my friend—I had been confiding in him, and asking his advice. How grateful I am to this man who took my tears and my face of fear seriously the day I left. He showed only empathy and kindness to my situation. He was also the one who called my father to tell him what had happened, and that he was trying to help get me safe. I am very sure my father is grateful for this man, too. Because this friend was a mutual friend of my predator's and mine, after he helped me leave he was approached by my predator. I am very sure my predator was able to persuade him that I was losing my mind and was unwell. This, after all, has been his whole defense since I left him—that I was mentally unwell and needed help. I am pretty sure this mutual friend has backed off from asking how I am doing, to checking in just once in a while, due to my predator. I am okay with that. He doesn't know the whole story. He doesn't know what my predator did to us after I left him. Harassing us, stalking our home, threatening his life, burning images of himself and me, posting half nude images of me on social media publicly, scaring our young child to the point our child was no longer comfortable being around him alone, and being ripped from our home by victim services for our safety. It's hard to see past someone who is so good at lying, and believing their lies are truth.

My dad. How scared I was to speak to my dad and tell him that the person he trusted with his daughter hurt her. My dad told me to get out. My dad, surprisingly, was calm. I think because I was so... not calm. I don't know if my dad believed me right away. I believe he knew I was scared to go home. I believe he knew I had to get away from my predator, but I don't know if he believed right away what my predator had actually done to me. I know when he was a kid, stuff happened to his family members, and being in a small town, they just never talked about it, and kept it hush hush. My dad was scared for me. He was scared that if I said anything to the police, I would only make it worse. He thought my predator would hurt me further. My dad believes me now. He believes I was sexually assaulted, he believes that had I not gone to the police the harassment would have been worse than worse. He believes in me and has stood by me.

My mom. From the moment she found out what was going on she stayed on the phone with me to ensure I got out of my home safely. She believed me as soon as I told her what happened. She was terrified I would go back to him. I told her I would not. It was hard for her because she knows most abused people return to their abuser a few times before being able to leave them for good. I just had to show her I meant I was not going back to him, ever. She has stood by my side right from the beginning— helping me find a place to live, making me feel safe to talk about the abuse I went through, making me feel safe to talk about my feelings, and reassuring me that I am not crazy. Checking on my boys and me daily, to make sure we are all safe. Helping me to understand that I am not the first person this has happened to, and that she was proud of me for having the strength to leave my predator, and to fight him to keep my voice. My mom stood with me at court to support me, to believe me, and to hug me after we found out the outcome of my predator's guilty plea.

My brother. My brother lives thousands of miles away and we never got along as kids, but his support and advice has meant the world to me. Knowing he believed me, too, was huge. I could not have had more support from my family than they gave me. They have amazed me with their strength through all this, too. It not only takes a toll on the family member or friend being abused, but on the supporters as well. They worry all the time. They stress over whether your predator will go to jail, and what will happen once he is released—what he could possibly do next. They stress for your kids' safety, and what will happen to them should something happen to you because of your predator. They stress over not being close enough to help more than they already are. They worry for your physical and mental health, and they worry for your life.

Friend after friend believed me when I told them what happened and showed them the messages between my predator and I. They believed the constant harassment, the constant stalking, and the fear I had for my safety, and my children's safety. They are there in ways they may not even realize. Words of encouragement have helped me to keep my head high, to keep fighting for my safety, and that of my children. Their words have lifted me when I felt hopeless about the constant battles in court. Their prayers helped me pray, too.

I chose to cut ties with "mutual friends" and friends my predator introduced me to. I chose to cut ties with his family members. I didn't want to leave myself open to more assaults or abuse from my predator through these people. Only they can decide what they feel is true. Only hearing one side of things makes it easier for them to sway their decisions one way. Knowing this made it easier for me to cut those ties. I chose not to post anything on any social media site for almost a year. I still am cautious about posting photos of myself and of my children. I have stuck to just liking others posts, and wishing happy birthdays. I didn't want to leave myself open to being found through a photo, or making a comment that would incriminate me. I wanted my voice to be heard, but only by the ones who wanted to hear it.

Leaving people behind us is never easy. Especially if you became friends, hung out, made future plans, and got along well. It's even harder letting go of the other children you cared for and helped raise. Cutting them off may seem to harsh and unfair. This is what I thought until my predator showed that there was no end to his abuse—from the time I went to get my first Emergency Protection Order and being told by that very Judge to go to the police, to the very last protection order that was granted. It wasn't easy. It got lonely, but I made sure to stay grounded. When I needed my family, I went to see them, or I told them I needed them. If I needed a friend, I knew who I could go to. I have many friends that I thankfully was able to go to, and am still able to go to.

Some of the words of encouragement that have helped me through this are "You are a really good mom," "You're a fighter—keep fighting for those kids," "I am so proud of you," "You're so strong," "You would make an amazing advocate for other people going through this," "You are a warrior," "You did the hardest part—you left him."

These words helped me. Hearing them helped me. My kids helped me, and I knew I had to keep fighting. I got discouraged at times because I just wanted to feel safe, and I wanted my kids to feel safe again. Sometimes I was frustrated that my predator seemed to gain the upper hand in court when he would gain an inch. I stayed focused. I did things the way I was supposed to. I called the police when I needed to, and I didn't let them talk me out of how I felt when they asked if maybe I was overreacting (only two of the officers I dealt with did this). I had lawyers who fought for my kids and my safety. I had fair Judges who listened to both sides of the story, and although it would have been easier to have just one Judge deal with every aspect in court, I had a great support system from family and friends, to my Domestic Violence Advocates from John Howard, and at the courthouse. I also learned I was my own and biggest advocate for myself. I didn't know this; I was told this along the way.

As much as I want my predator to see that I no longer fear him, I do. I have every right to fear the person who abused me, made me fearful in our home, who physically hurt me by sexually assaulting me nightly, who raped me, who tried to mentally break me by continuing to criminally harass me, stalk me, and embarrass me on social media, someone who I believe hurt our son, and who allegedly hurt others before me. We all have the right to fear that he would do it again, given the chance. I heard over and over again from the police, from my lawyers, from friends and family, that my predator is narcissistic. I didn't know what this meant. I googled it after speaking to a therapist on the phone during an intake interview, and she also believed this term described my predator's behaviour. I see it now.

He always took my money, spending it as he pleased; he contributed very little, made me feel bad for things I should never have felt bad for, like going out with friends or working late. He made me feel guilty for not doing something he wanted me to, like having sex when I was extremely ill, for accusing me of cheating, for continuing his abuse in court by adjourning every hearing to try to gain control back, to trying to get me to defend myself on social media when he made hundreds of posts for all to see. I see how scary it was, and how much worse it could have been. I still believe he wouldn't have hesitated to take my life had he had the opportunity to do so. Had I not gotten protection orders or had police involvement at every mistake he made. I don't regret leaving him. I don't have guilt. I don't regret calling the police or going to court and asking for help. I am grateful for the resources I was able to use, and continue to use today.

So many things could have happened. I am slowly learning not to dwell on the "what if's," and starting to get back into living my life again. I am still cautious of my surroundings, but I am not totally fearful. To me, it's important for people to know what happened to us. I encourage my children to talk about it. I don't want my kids' voices taken away by what our predator did to us. I want them to be strong and courageous, and to speak their truth. I know my kids are strong. I see they are resilient, but I never want them to feel like they cannot talk about their experience. I was not the only one who went through this—they did, too.

I hope that being able to speak about our experiences will somehow help someone else. I want us all to fight. I want to fight to end all types of domestic violence against men, women, and children. We need to take back control, and keep this from becoming the norm. Abuse is not okay. Controlling people is not okay. Hitting, kicking, biting, stabbing, killing, sexually assaulting, raping, stalking, manipulating, and making us fearful for our lives, and trying to silence abuse is not okay. I hope one day this will change, and that there will be harsher punishments for those who abuse others, and I hope that it becomes easier to prove their guilt. Until then, I will keep fighting for myself, for my kids, and for anyone else who has or will go through this.

Acknowledgements

I WOULD TRULY like to thank my family and friends who have stuck by my side, believing me when I told them what had happened to me, and helping me move forward with my life—I most certainly could not have done it without you all. To my advocates and lawyers, thank you for your patience and guidance through this unfortunate ordeal, and for fighting alongside me. To the Edmonton Police Services and the officers who dealt with this case, thank you so very much for understanding that when I called, it was because I was in dire need of your help. Thank you for helping with ending the domestic violence my children and I had to endure.

Thank you to the many others who contributed to helping me and my children heal—the John Howard Society of Edmonton, the Family Center, the Boys and Girls Club, the Sexual Assault Center of Edmonton, CASA, the Mental Health and Wellness Center of Edmonton, DVCAP and of course, my many lawyers and doctors.

CPSIA information can be obtained
at www.ICGtesting.com
Printed in the USA
LVHW101740040522
717946LV00011B/1606